DATE DUE

Lexington Studies in Political Communication

Series Editor: Robert E. Denton, Jr., Virginia Tech University

This series encourages focused work examining the role and function of communication in the realm of politics including campaigns and elections, media, and political institutions.

Recent Titles in This Series

The Political Blame Game in American Democracy

The Political Blame Game in American Democracy

Mark Hickson III and Larry Powell

LEXINGTON BOOKS
Lanham • Boulder • New York • London

Published by Lexington Books
An imprint of The Rowman & Littlefield Publishing Group, Inc.
4501 Forbes Boulevard, Suite 200, Lanham, Maryland 20706
www.rowman.com

Unit A, Whitacre Mews, 26-34 Stannary Street, London SE11 4AB

British Library Cataloguing in Publication Information Available

Library of Congress Cataloging-in-Publication Data

Names: Hickson, Mark, author. | Powell, Larry, 1948– author.
Title: The political blame game in American democracy / Mark Hickson III and Larry Powell.
Description: Lanham, Maryland : Lexington Books, 2017. | Series: Lexington studies in political communication | Includes bibliographical references and index.
Identifiers: LCCN 2017036924 (print) | LCCN 2017039877 (ebook) | ISBN 9781498545464 (electronic) | ISBN 9781498545457 (hardcover : alk. paper)
Subjects: LCSH: Political culture—United States. | Polarization (Social sciences)—Political aspects—United States. | Blame—Political aspects—United States. | Responsibility—Political aspects—United States. | United States—Politics and government—1945–1989. | United States—Politics and government—1989-
Classification: LCC JK1726 (ebook) | LCC JK1726 .H53 2017 (print) | DDC 320.973--dc23
LC record available at https://lccn.loc.gov/2017036924

∞™ The paper used in this publication meets the minimum requirements of American National Standard for Information Sciences Permanence of Paper for Printed Library Materials, ANSI/NISO Z39.48-1992.

Printed in the United States of America

Contents

ONE

In the *Beginning*

Two three-year-olds are caught having an argument when their mother enters the room. "Who spilled this juice?" "I didn't do it," innocently answers the first. "I didn't do it!" replies the second. The mother knows that she didn't do it. Instead of becoming like a policeman, the mother hides behind the corner and observes. Then the children return to their arguing. "It was your fault," announces the first. "No, you pushed me." "You spit on me first." "You took my teddy bear." And so it goes. In their subsequent argument, they may return to the last argument. "You got me in trouble, so I tore up your teddy bear." This sequence of events should sound familiar to parents, but it also closely resembles what we have observed in political America over the past 70 years. If we substitute "Republican" for child one, "Democrat" for child two, and the "American public" for mother, this is where we find ourselves. Everything we know about politics, we should have learned in nursery school.

The similarities between young children and America's two dominant political parties are significant. The primary differences are the topics that create conflict. In politics, the topics include: consumerism, narcissism, religion, and fear (Kitchens & Powell, 2015). *Consumerism* relates to the notion that America has an economy that is dependent on its citizens buying things and ideally having others around the world purchase them as well. Consumerism is inherent in a capitalistic state. It relates to who may own the economic resources in such a state. *Narcissism* concerns patriotism and the notion that the United States is the best country in the world. We note this concept when we watch the Olympics. Many fans disregard the athletic excellence and prowess of Cuban boxers or distance runners from Africa. The issue in the Olympics is how many medals the United States' athletes receive. *Religion* focuses on the similarities and differences among Americans. While the First Amendment to the

1

Constitution specifically disallows our country to create a state religion, the members of individual denominations believe that their religious views are superior to all others. These religions establish the moral and ethical values for American society. *Fear* embraces all of the other three. In political campaigns, fear is the central motivator. Anything that may cause the loss of any one of the other three can be used to motivate Americans to change. We must fear natural disasters, other countries and terrorist groups attempting to change our way of life, and those who might limit our freedoms.

Our purpose in this book is to sort out these childish arguments. The path is somewhat cumbersome and obviously depends on where we start. We could go back to the beginning of the country with the details of the Democratic-Republicans and the Federalists. For the readers' benefit we will not do that. However, a couple of sentences about our country's founders might be important. The Democratic-Republicans were led by Thomas Jefferson and James Madison and the party was strongest in the agrarian South, especially Virginia. The Federalists were led by Alexander Hamilton, who supported a strong central government. The Federalists' most significant supporters were from the Northeast. Thus, one party was pro-central government (the Federalists) and the other favored states' rights (Ferling, 2014). The issue of power division between the central government and the states was still with us into the 19th century. Two constitutional provisions were negotiated regarding the states. The House of Representatives would be based on each state's population. But every single state, regardless of population, would have two senators (Bordewich, 2016). The addition of the 10th Amendment gave the states any rights not allocated to the federal government in the Constitution (Jones, 2010).

This issue, federal versus state, has been with us in one way or another ever since (Epstein & Greve, 2007). The disagreement may have been more than a simple argument. In large measure, one can say that it was a significant, contributing cause of the Civil War. The states' rights issue was favorable for the South and most slaves were owned by southerners. The agricultural economy was much more central to living in the South. The South was more rural. Even before the "super beltway" from Washington to Baltimore to Philadelphia to New York City to Boston, a separation existed between the mostly rural South and the urban Northeast.

Jefferson was a Virginia plantation owner and Hamilton was a New York lawyer and banker. As new states were admitted to the union, decisions about adding states were based primarily on one factor: slave state or free state? Each time a state was admitted, two more senators were added. The "new" states, mostly from the West, were less populous. Their power in the House of Representatives would be negligible in the immediate context. The compromise from the beginning continued.

When a free state was added, a slave state was added. The process went on and on. The original Constitution mentioned slavery only on the issue of the census, in which it stated that slaves were to be counted as 3/5th of a person. Of course, the census is the measure of how many members a state has in the House of Representatives, which leads to how many electoral votes a state has, which results in the more populous states having a greater influence in determining who is elected president. By counting the slaves as only 3/5ths of a person, most of the southern states were at a disadvantage regarding the census and consequently the number of delegates to the House of Representatives and to the Electoral College.

The slave versus free issue became a state versus federal issue. The conflict was an agricultural versus a non-agricultural debate. It was a state-versus-state issue in terms of power that became a rural-versus-city issue (Richards, 2000). Many of the issues in place today naturally follow from this line that started with the Jeffersonians and the Federalists (see Table 1.1).

We could start with the Civil War, although that may be a bit too far back as well. Instead, we start with the death of FDR. Franklin Delano Roosevelt, a Democrat, served as president of the United States for more than 12 years. Had he lived, he would have served for at least sixteen. He inherited our nation's worst economic depression in 1933, and in 1941 went to war against Japan, Germany, and Italy in what was arguably the most gruesome war in the history of mankind with more than 60 million people killed (Smith, 2007).

Within two years of Roosevelt's death, Congress voted to approve the 22nd Amendment to the Constitution to ensure that no one would ever serve as president for that long again (Amar, 2005). Truman was grandfathered in and could have run again. The issue was moot until Ronald Reagan hinted that he might want to run for a third term after completing his second in 1988 (Sutherland, 2008). The release of information about Reagan's Alzheimer's disease put an end to that possibility. The fact that a constitutional amendment would be required may have had a hand in it as well.

Roosevelt's lengthy administration took away the power balance between the parties. While many praised FDR for getting us out of the Great Depression, he was also considered a dictator of sorts by others. In fact he probably had more individual authority than any president since

Table 1.1.   Divisions in the Country on States' Rights.

For/Against States' Rights	Pro or Anti-Slavery	Rural vs. Urban	Region
For States' Rights	Pro-Slavery	Rural	South
For central government	Anti-Slavery	Urban	Northeast

George Washington. He created social and economic programs with his New Deal. One of the things that the New Deal did was to make the federal government a major employer. FDR even tried unsuccessfully to pack the Supreme Court via adding additional justices instead of waiting for some of them to die or retire.

In general, though, there appears to be some kind of underlying assumption that the presidency should switch about every eight years from one party to another, a precedent that began with George Washington. The statistics largely support this in reality (see Table 1.2).

One might quibble about portions of years in individual cases, but the fact remains that since 1945, the United States has had virtually an equal number of years of Democrat and Republican presidential administrations. It may not seem that way in the midst of a president's sixth year in office, but in fact it is the case.

If one were to read about the 22nd Amendment, he or she would find that George Washington and the early presidents voluntarily sought to end their presidencies after eight years. But the idea of creating a Constitutional Amendment to prevent a person from running for more than eight years did not occur until months after FDR's death. Did FDR *start* all of this conflict because he was elected four times? Does this mean that the Republicans *started* it by passing the 22nd Amendment? The probability is that the perception of who started it depends on whether one looks at the issue(s) from a Democratic perspective or a Republican perspective. As a sidebar, no other elected, federal office has a term limit.

Table 1.2.   Presidential Administrations, 1945–2016.

Years	# of Years	President	Political Party	Cumulative Score
1945–1952	6 [+2 FDR]	Harry Truman	Democrat	D, 8–0
1953–1960	8	Dwight Eisenhower	Republican	R, 8–8
1961–1963	2	John F. Kennedy	Democrat	D, 10–8
1963–1968	6	Lyndon Johnson	Democrat	D, 16–8
1969–1974	6	Richard Nixon	Republican	D-16–14
1974–1976	2	Gerald Ford	Republican	Tie, 16–16
1977–1980	4	Jimmy Carter	Democrat	D, 20–16
1981–1988	8	Ronald Reagan	Republican	R, 24–20
1989–1992	4	George H. W. Bush	Republican	R, 28–20
1993–2000	8	Bill Clinton	Democrat	Tie, 28–28
2001–2008	8	George W. Bush	Republican	R, 36–28
2009–2016	8	Barack Obama	Democrat	Tie, 36–36

THE TRUMAN ADMINISTRATION

Harry Truman was hardly Franklin Roosevelt's first choice for vice president. FDR had other vice presidents before, but they were not Truman. For one, Roosevelt was Ivy League-educated. Truman did not hold a college degree. Truman himself was reluctant to take the job, feeling that the "meaningless position" would only lose him a vote in the Senate. He had been a U. S. Senator from Missouri for more than a term and had gotten used to having a vote. Nevertheless, as it turned out, his reign as VP was short. In fact, the Democrats selected him because they did not want Henry Wallace to continue as Roosevelt's vice president because they feared that FDR's health was deteriorating. The Democrats were concerned that Wallace might be too unpredictable. The war was still going on when the nomination process took place in 1944 and unpredictability was not what anyone wanted (McCullough, 1992).

Just a month into Truman's first term, the war in Europe ended. But the war continued in Asia. It was not until August (three months later) that Truman ordered atomic bombs be dropped on Hiroshima and Nagasaki (Bartlett & O'Connor, 2015). The bombing was accepted by Americans at the time, although polls undertaken decades later were not as agreeable about whether the decision was a good one. In any case, Truman justified the decision as saving more lives than its alternative, i.e., continued ground fighting with no end in sight.

By the end of 1945, the United States had provided its support for the United Nations (Meisler, 1995). The international organization was supposed to be stronger than its predecessor, the League of Nations, that Woodrow Wilson was unable to convince Americans to join. The obvious ineffectiveness of the League was confirmed by the creation of Nazi Germany and World War II. Public and political criticism of the decision was apparent when the organization was formed and remains so today. Much of the criticism involved the idea that the United States would have less power to decide its own foreign policy and control in waging war.

Less than four years later, the Soviet Union had its own nuclear weapons. Joseph Stalin, the general secretary of the Communist Party in the Soviet Union, had been suspicious of his allies' (especially the United States and Great Britain) even during the war. Although the Soviets had begun a program of nuclear armament as the war was continuing, it was not until 1949 that the Soviet project was complete. If the Cold War had not begun immediately after Germany's surrender, it certainly had begun in 1949 (Zubok, 2009).

Truman ran for election as president for the first time in 1948. His Republican opponent, Thomas Dewey, was governor of New York State. Dewey was considered a moderate Republican who supported big business. He was also known as an internationalist. In many ways, Dewey's Republican Party resembled Hamilton's Federalist Party. Dewey had run against FDR in 1944 and was Roosevelt's fiercest competitor. It was FDR's closest victory. In 1948, the pollsters predicted that Dewey would defeat Truman, but in what is still considered the biggest upset in presidential election history up to that time, Truman won (Pietrusza, 2011).

One of the reasons that Truman was expected to lose was that a third party had nominated a candidate for president. The feeling was that the Dixiecrat Party, led by Strom Thurmond from South Carolina, would take away votes from Truman (Frederickson, 2001). The Dixiecrat Party was a segregationist party following the thought that "The South shall rise again." To some extent, the Dixiecrats projected an image that the Civil War was not over. Despite the fact that the Dixiecrats didn't have enough electoral votes to change the election, they did receive 39 votes, from Alabama, Mississippi, South Carolina, and Louisiana, as well as one of Tennessee's votes.

The Speaker of the House of Representatives between 1939 and 1961, with the exception of two years, was Sam Rayburn, a Democrat from Texas (Hardeman & Bacon, 1987). From 1933 to 1953, with the exception of two years, the Democrats also controlled the Senate. The most notable of the Senate leaders of the time was Lyndon B. Johnson, who was also from Texas. In general, southerners maintained strength in Congress, primarily because the voters in southern states realized the importance of an incumbent having seniority. Thurmond, in fact, had been one of those powerful Democrats.

As we view this second southern rebellion, we find a host of inconsistencies. The southern Congressmen, who were all white men, had chosen the Democratic Party for reasons unrelated to race relations of the time. The selection of the Democratic Party was actually a rebellion against the Republicans and Abraham Lincoln, the man who had freed the slaves. The fact that the Congressmen gained political power by serving in the party was merely icing on the cake.

In a sense, the opposition to the southern power brokers was two-fold. One was the eastern establishment of Republicans like Taft. The other was the eastern moderate establishment in the Democratic Party.

Truman's actions primarily motivated the Dixiecrats to emerge. President Truman had integrated the military services, eliminated the poll tax, and signed a Fair Employment Practices Act. All of these actions were felt by the southerners to be a slap in the face. They were beginning to believe that they were fighting a second civil war and might be losing once again. Thirty-five senators and representatives from the South met to select their presidential and vice presidential candidates in Birmingham, Alabama. The Thurmond ticket received only 29 electoral votes. Georgia and Texas did not vote for the Dixiecrats.

The issue of race remained the elephant in the room. Southern politicians continued to use extreme racist rhetoric in their own states though not necessarily in the national spotlight. The elimination of the poll tax had knocked out one barrier for preventing African Americans from voting, but other barriers still kept many blacks from the voting booths. Most notable was a literacy test which was a requirement in most states.

In foreign policy, there remained a fear of the Soviet Union. The House Un-American Activities Committee (HUAC) investigated those who might threaten the security of the country. While the committee started out investigating Nazis, they began looking at Communists after World War II. One of the members of the Committee was Richard M. Nixon, a young congressman from California. He helped investigate a case against Alger Hiss, who was accused of being a Soviet spy. As the issue moved forward, Hiss was convicted of two counts of perjury and served more than three years in prison. This may have been the most notable of the "communists" who had served in the government. The most publicized cases of the HUAC, though, were in Hollywood, where many in the film industry were accused of being members of the Communist Party. Many were ultimately blacklisted from the cinema business. The early work of the HUAC was a prelude to the McCarthy hearings in the Senate. The HUAC was also a predominant force in the rhetoric of fear. Truman himself condemned the committee itself as un-American (Bentley, 1971).

The witnesses included Walt Disney, an entertainment executive, who provided a list of potential Hollywood people who might be communist-connected. The president of the Screen Actors Guild, Ronald Reagan, indicated that some members of the Guild might be so connected, especially those who were pro-labor union.

Another end-of-war plan involved the creation of Israel, which was carved out of Palestinian territory. The United Nations developed the plan. Almost immediately, Palestinian forces began firing on the new state. While this was not a problem for the United States at that time, the "Israeli Question," or perhaps more aptly, the "Middle East Question" would come to haunt America.

Meanwhile, in 1948, seemingly hypocritical approaches were taken. The Marshall Plan to rebuild some of the countries devastated by World War II was put into place. However, Truman put in place a peacetime selective service system, which irritated the Soviet Union. The next year, Truman ordered research on a hydrogen bomb to counteract the Soviet Union's atomic bomb (Bernstein, 1984).

Much of the domestic policy between 1948 and 1950 involved trying to get the veterans settled. The foreign policy was directed against the Soviet Union. The two general policies, it seems, were agreeable to both American political parties. The veterans' benefits allowed much of the country to become better off economically. Disputes over the division of Germany, Berlin in particular, and the ideological concerns about communism continued to bring fear in the international realm. The Soviet Union was also expanding its geographical presence.

In 1950, there arose a need to call on those soldiers who were part of the Selective Service System when the Korean War began (Flynn, 1985). Nuclear testing began in a Nevada test site. Julius and Ethel Rosenberg were convicted of espionage and sentenced to death, charged with providing information to the Soviet Union about the atomic bomb. In May of 1951, congressional hearings involved the firing of General Douglas MacArthur whom Truman had dismissed. The Cold War was in full force, and one of the nation's hero military figures was no longer around. In 1952, Harry Truman announced that he would not run for re-election.

A WAR HERO RETURNS

In the election of 1952, General Dwight Eisenhower, another of the war heroes, ran as the Republican candidate for president. The "solid South," returned to its selection of voting for Democrats. Adlai Stevenson, the Democratic candidate, won the states from North Carolina to Louisiana and Arkansas. Only Virginia, Florida, Tennessee, and Texas aligned themselves with the General. Kentucky and West Virginia were the only other states joining the southerners in voting Democrat. Stevenson didn't even win his home state, Illinois. Stevenson selected John Sparkman as his vice presidential running mate. Because Sparkman was from Alabama, perhaps Stevenson felt that the geographical balance would assure them of southern support. So despite running away from the party as the Dixiecrats in 1948, the southerners returned to the anti-Lincoln party, although the voting remained split with many of the votes going to Eisenhower.

The First Eisenhower Year

The next year, the world was stunned by the death of Joseph Stalin in the Soviet Union. From an American viewpoint, Stalin was a terrible dictator but was at least predictable. The shakeup in the Kremlin created a vacuum. In the final outcome, the leader would be Nikita Khrushchev. An agreement was made as regarded Korea. Korea would be divided into north and south regions. A demilitarized zone was created between the two Koreas. The agreement did not solve many problems, and issues with North Korea remain today. An American presence remains in South Korea.

On the domestic side, Eisenhower appointed Earl Warren as chief justice of the Supreme Court. Eisenhower thought that Warren would appeal to the eastern liberals in the party as well as the "law-and-order" conservatives. Warren, the three-time governor of California, had been somewhat of a pawn in the 1952 presidential election. Warren's running for the presidency himself as a favorite son was usurped by fellow Californian Richard Nixon. Warren had expected a brokered convention, which did not occur. Nixon was selected as the vice-presidential candidate and was ultimately elected vice president. The Warren Court decisions would eventually become a significant problem for Eisenhower, who later stated that selecting Warren for the Supreme Court position was the worst decision he ever made (Belknap & Warren, 2005).

1954

Eisenhower publicly stated his "domino" theory in regard to foreign policy in 1954. He used the term at a press conference in which he stated that if one country yields to communist influence, that action is likely to bring down other countries as well. The theory was directed at what was going on in Indo-China. The French were defeated in Vietnam.

Shortly after becoming chief justice, Warren and the Warren Court ruled on *Brown versus Board of Education* (Topeka, Kansas). The case involved whether states could have "separate but equal" schools for African Americans. The 1954 ruling was that they could not. The decision was not only applicable to the state of Kansas but also to all of the states, which most notably included southern states. The result was that black and white children would be required to attend public schools together. Certainly this decision was the "last straw" for southern politicians who had been re-fighting the Civil War for almost a century (Rubin, 2016). On top of the previous decisions to eliminate the poll tax, many southerners were convinced that black Americans were gaining power and that the white establishment was losing it. Now, the court had even interfered in a state's educational systems, which historically had been viewed as a state's right. Despite the ruling, though, implementation of the Warren Court decision would take almost two decades. But the public flak over the appointment of Warren began almost immediately, especially in the South where highways were filled with billboards imploring the impeachment of Warren. The intended balance of power among the Congress, the president, and the Supreme Court had left the Court behind at least until Warren became the chief justice.

Foreign Relations

Chiang Kai-Shek was the leader of the Republic of China. The separation of the tiny island of Formosa (Taiwan), though, generated a new foreign policy obligation for the United States. Along with Israel, the United States began expanding its influence and its obligations. Any problems between Nationalist China and Communist China would involve the United States (Rushdorff, 1981). Since an agreement had been made with China regarding North and South Korea, the new Chinese state made policy in Asia more difficult. This was especially the case with a weakened Japan that had lost the war (see Table 1.3).

America's foreign policy obligations increased from the pre-war allies (United Kingdom, France, the Soviet Union) to concerns all over the world. Because of a number of factors, the Soviet Union was no longer seen as an ally.

In Washington, Joseph McCarthy, a Republican Senator from Wisconsin, began Congressional hearings on Communism as somewhat of a follow-up to the House Un-Americans Affairs Committee hearings. The committee hearings lasted 36 days, during which there were concerns about Communists in the federal government, especially the U. S. Army. The hearings were eventually perceived as unfair, biased, and dictatorial. McCarthy was attacked for his approach by several Columbia Broadcasting System (CBS) journalists led by Edward R. Murrow (Wershba, 1979).

The United States had supported the French with money to fight in Indo-China from 1950. But in 1955, Eisenhower approved sending military advisors to Vietnam. The contingenct was less than 1,000, which remained about the same throughout Eisenhower's administration.

In Montgomery, Alabama, a black woman, Rosa Parks, refused the orders of a bus driver who demanded that she give up her seat to a white passenger.

1956

In 1956, the "solid South" remained with the Democrats, at least *mostly*. The voting was similar to 1952, except that Louisiana voted for Eisenhower, and Missouri joined the southern alignment. Alabama did cast one vote for a local jurist who was a noted segregationist. Eisenhower defeated Stevenson in a rematch in which the Democrats were supported only by the southern group of states.

Eisenhower signed federal highway legislation, making way for the interstate highway system as a mechanism for national security.

Table 1.3.   Foreign Obligations after WW II and Their Source.

Source	Country	Year
World War II	Japan, Federal Republic of Germany	1945–present
Creation of Israel	Israel	1948–present
Korean Agreement	South Korea	1953–present
Creation of Republic of China	Republic of China	1949–present

EISENHOWER'S SECOND ADMINISTRATION

In his first year of his second administration, Eisenhower articulated what became known as "The Eisenhower Doctrine," wherein the United States would provide economic support for countries threatened by outsiders, especially in the Middle East. He noted that our country had certain interests in the Middle East, not the least of which was oil. Eisenhower's main concern was the friendliness between the Soviet Union and Egypt. The relationship did not last, and our policy was shifted to one of accommodation with Egyptian leader Gamal Abdel Nasser. At one point, Nasser had closed the Suez Canal, but he then re-opened it.

In October, the Soviet Union launched a satellite, *Sputnik*, and fears arose in the United States that the Soviets' technology was surpassing that of other countries in the world. (Killian, 1977). In part, there was a concern about how satellites could be used as part of military arsenal. A month later, Eisenhower suffered a stroke.

A group of rebels in Cuba began making plans to overthrow the government of Fulgencio Batista.

Most notably during this time, Little Rock Central (Arkansas) High School was racially integrated in accordance with the implementation of the *Brown versus Board of Education* decision by the Supreme Court. Eisenhower and Governor Orval Faubus confronted each other. Local police were unable to handle mobs trying to prevent the black students from entering. Ultimately, the president ordered Army regulars into Little Rock to assure that the Supreme Court's order was implemented. It was only the first of several interactions between the federal government and state governments regarding integration of the races in public schools (Beals, 1995).

1958–1959

Eisenhower signed documents to make Alaska the 49th state of the union. After much fighting in Havana and elsewhere in Cuba Fidel Castro became the leader of one of our closest neighbors. In March of 1959, Hawaii was added as the 50th state of the union. In April, the National Aeronautics and Space Administration (NASA) selected the first men who would potentially become American astronauts in space. At Eisenhower's invitation, Soviet premier Nikita Khrushchev and his wife paid a visit to the United States.

1960

Any attempt to improve relations between the United States and the Soviet Union was spoiled when an American reconnaissance plane, the U-2, flew over the Soviet Union. The plane was shot down by a Soviet missile. The plane was completely destroyed, but the Russians captured the pilot, Francis Gary Powers. The incident brought the Cold War to a much higher temperature. The final outcome was an apology by the United States and an exchange of prisoners which returned Powers to the States. Rudolf Abel, a Soviet intelligence officer, was returned to Russia.

The term for lame duck Dwight Eisenhower was almost over. In July, the Republicans met in Chicago and nominated Richard Nixon, Eisenhower's vice president during both terms, for President. Henry Cabot Lodge, from Massachusetts, was the vice presidential nominee. In the same month, in a competitive race in Los Angeles, the Democrats selected John F. Kennedy, a senator from Massachusetts. A new generation was about to take over the country.

REMNANTS OF THE WAR

The first 15 years following World War II brought substantial changes in the composition of the United States. In terms of foreign policy commitments, our country remained close allies with France and particularly Great Britain. The Soviet Union's assistance in defeating Nazi Germany, though, merely created a new enemy of sorts. The Marxist–Leninist ideology was feared by conservative Americans, who became suspicious of not only the Soviet Union but also of Americans who subscribed to the ideology. The United States forged new commitments to Taiwan, as we had an obligation to protect it from China. The same was true of South Korea. There was an obvious vacuum of power in Asia, since Japan had lost the war, and the United States had no desire to remilitarize its former enemy. The impact of Eisenhower sending military advisors to Vietnam was yet to be known.

In the Middle East, America supported the creation of the new Jewish state, Israel. In addition, though, we supported other countries in the region because of the vast oil supply held there. Concerns about America spreading itself too thinly began to emerge.

Domestically, the racial integration of the country was occurring. The poll tax had been eliminated as a mechanism for the southern states to prevent black Americans from voting, although they held onto literacy tests to continue the election fight against blacks. The minority blacks, though, were becoming more adamant about their rights. In *Brown versus Board of Education*, the Supreme Court virtually ended (at least in theory) segregated public schools. A black woman in Montgomery, Alabama, had shown contempt to a city bus driver in what would become a pattern. Schools in Little Rock, Arkansas, ended segregation, illustrating the seriousness with which the federal government took the *Brown* decision. All of this was in opposition to the states' rights perspective held by southern, conservative Democrats.

In 1960, the southern Democrats stood by their anti-Lincoln roots. Obviously, Eisenhower was merely another Republican who was trying to force the black population into the mainstream. The idea was obvious through Eisenhower's appointment of Earl Warren and the federal troops being brought into Little Rock. The sole rebellion of the Dixiecrats in one election had not helped them in their battle for their states nor for their "rights."

CONCLUSIONS

FDR created a precedent, one that Republicans never wanted to encounter again, when he was elected president for four consecutive terms. The consequences for Truman as the successor involved having a less than cooperative legislature. The victory in World War II placed the United States as a major power in the world. In essence, it helped create a narcissistic idea that remains today—that America could protect the rest of the world. America was seen as "the" power. The Soviet Union, however, had the same idea. American entries into Israel, Taiwan, Vietnam, and Korea expanded the locus of control for the United States.

Eisenhower's positions on civil rights, frequently in opposition to states' rights, created an encounter within the country. The appointment of Earl Warren and the integration of the Little Rock schools supported southerners' feelings that the Republicans were continuing Lincoln's legacy.

Overall, the nation was still functioning, and compromise was still possible among the participants. Fear was a major factor in the nation, with citizens having to deal with the fear of a potential nuclear war with the Soviet Union, but the parties still sought out compromise during the process of governing. The seeds for dysfunction had been sown, but they had not yet grown to full size.

REFERENCES

Amar, A. M. (2005). *America's constitution: A biography.* New York: Random House.

Bartlett, M., & O'Connor, R. (2015). *Hiroshima & Nagasaki.* Carwoola, Australia: Odyssey Books.

Beals, M. (1995). *Warriors don't cry: A searing memoir of the battle to integrate Little Rock.* New York: Simon & Schuster.

Belknap, M. R., & Warren, E. (2005). *The Supreme Court under Earl Warren, 1953–1969.* Columbia: University of South Carolina Press.

Bentley, E. (1971). *Thirty years of treason: excerpts from hearings before the House Committee on Un-American Activities, 1938–1968.* New York: Viking.

Bernstein, B. J. (1984). Truman and the H-Bomb. *Bulletin of the Atomic Scientists, 40*(3), 12–18.

Bordewich, F. M. (2016). *The first Congress: How James Madison, George Washington and a group of extraordinary men invented the government.* New York: Simon & Schuster.

Epstein, R. A., & Greve, M. S. (2007). *Federal preemption: States' power, national interests.* Washington, DC: American Enterprise Institute for Public Policy Research.

Ferling, J. (2014). *Jefferson and Hamilton: The rivalry that forged a nation.* New York: Bloomsbury Press.

Flynn, G. Q. (1985). *Lewis B. Hershey, Mr. Selective Service.* Chapel Hill: University of North Carolina Press.

Frederickson, K. (2001). *The Dixiecrat revolt and the end of the solid South, 1932–1968.* Chapel Hill: University of North Carolina Press.

Hardeman, D. B., & Bacon, D. C. (1987). *Rayburn: A biography.* Austin: Texas Monthly Press.

Killian, J. R. (1977). *Sputnik, scientists, and Eisenhower: A memoir of the first special assistant to the president for science and technology.* Cambridge, MA: MIT Press.

Jones, A. (2010). *Gateway to liberty: The constitutional power of the 10th amendment.* Braselton, GA: American Vision.

Kitchens, J., & Powell, L. (2015). *The four pillars of democracy.* Lanham, MD: Lexington.

McCullough, D. (1992). *Truman.* New York: Simon & Schuster.

Meisler, S. (1995). *United Nations: A history.* New York: Grove Press.

Pietrusza, D. (2011). *1948: Harry Truman's improbable victory and the year that transformed America.* New York: Union Square Press.

Richards, L. L. (2000). *The slave power: The free North and Southern domination, 1780–1860.* Baton Rouge: Louisiana State University Press.

Rubin, S. G. (2016). *Brown v. Board of Education: A fight for simple justice.* New York: Holiday House.

Rushkoff, B. C. (1981). Eisenhower, Dulles and the Quemoy–Matsu Crisis, 1954–1955. *Political Science Quarterly, 96*(3), 465–480.

Smith, J. E. (2007). *FDR.* New York: Random House.

Sutherland, J. B. (2008). *Ronald Reagan (Up close).* New York: Random House.

Wershba, J. (1979). "Murrow vs. McCarthy: See It Now." New York: *New York Times Magazine,* March 4.

Zubok, V. M. (2009). *A failed empire: The Soviet Union in the Cold War from Stalin to Gorbachev.* Chapel Hill: University of North Carolina Press.

TWO

1960: Kennedy versus Nixon

The biggest event that most political junkies remember from the 1960 campaign was the first televised debate, an event that popular culture argues played a key role in Kennedy's winning the election. Others argue that Kennedy's speech in Houston, in which he addressed concerns about his Catholic faith, was a key moment. But there were two other factors that may have been more important, particularly in the long run. First were the activities of a Democratic consultant named Dick Tuck, a man who did his best to sabotage Nixon's election campaign. Nixon's hatred of Tuck eventually led the Republican to form his own "dirty tricks" squad in 1972, leading to the Watergate debacle. Second, Kennedy won the election because he won the state of Illinois, albeit by an extremely small margin. That victory was likely due to voter fraud in Chicago. Nixon could have challenged the outcome, but decided it was in the best interest of the country not to engage in a legal battle. Still, his resentment seemed to have triggered some of his later behavior in 1968 and 1972.

THE 1960 DEBATE

Richard Nixon came into the 1960 presidential campaign as the only professional who had triumphantly used the power of television. In the fall of 1952, he defended himself against corruption charges by going on television to deliver his "Checkers" speech, a speech that was largely credited with saving his political career. However, the public had gone eight years without an additional display of the power of the medium. The only political messages that appeared on television during those intervening years were messages paid for by the candidates themselves. Further, there had never been an instance in which both presidential candidates stood on stage together in front of TV cameras (Lehner, 2011;

Minow, Martin & Mitchell, 1973). No one truly understood the power of free television time until 1960 (White, 2009). By the time that first debate was over, Wedley (2010) argued that the debate had "fundamentally political campaigns, television media and American political history" (19).

Many pundits of the day credited Kennedy's strong performance in his one-on-one debates with Nixon as the deciding factor in a close election. There were justifications for such an argument. Kennedy was a more media-friendly candidate than was Nixon. The television camera liked the young senator from Massachusetts, and he looked better and more relaxed on camera than did Nixon. Nixon, in contrast, participated in the first debate while nursing a painful knee injury. That injury contributed to him looking uncomfortable on camera. And, even though many observers believed that Nixon was better informed on policy positions, Kennedy came out looking best on camera. Further, most voters watched the debates. There were, after all, only three broadcast channels at the time, and all three aired the debates. As a result, more than 55 percent of all voters saw all of the debates and 80 percent saw parts of at least one (Kraus, 2001).

The first, and most crucial, debate was held in Chicago after both parties had gone through an extended round of negotiations regarding the rules and procedures for their appearances (Self, 2005). The broadcast of the debates hinged on both sides agreeing to a solution to Section 315 of the Communications Act of 1934, which required equal time for all candidates, including independent and third party candidates (Stanton, 2000). Nixon arrived about 15 minutes ahead of Kennedy, but "looked haggard and pale" while Kennedy looked like an "athlete come to receive his wreath of laurel" (Mlodinow, 2013, 138). By today's standards, the debate was civil and focused on issues, with no attempts at humor by either candidate (Rhea, 2012) and no effort to turn it into a reality television show as is common in today's politics (Halton, 2016). Instead, the debate focused more on positive claims by the candidates (Benoit & Harthcock, 1999) while setting standards for politeness for future debates (Dailey, Hinck & Hinck, 2007). Mehltretter Drury and Herbeck (2016) noted that the debate "helped to define—and continues to shape—how we remember two of the politicians who shaped postwar America" (187).

The candidates discussed issues with points and counterpoints, most of which turned out to be irrelevant by the time Kennedy took office. Still most popular observers believe that Kennedy handled the television medium much better than did Nixon. Schneider (2000) expressed the common opinion when he wrote that "Kennedy won because he looked better than Nixon on television" (3210). White (2009) went into a little more detail, arguing that the debate was seen as a tie by those who heard it on radio, but that Kennedy was the clear winner among those who watched it on television. In a tight election, that might have been enough to give Kennedy an electoral win.

Today, the event is featured in exhibits at the presidential libraries of both Kennedy and Nixon, but the two exhibits take different angles on the debate (Drury & Herbeck, 2016). Nixon's exhibit downplays the importance of the debate, while the Kennedy exhibit argues that Kennedy won "because of his cool demeanor, his confidence, and his mastery of the issues" (187). The importance of the debate for Kennedy may have been best expressed by Kennedy himself after the election. When asked if he could have won without a great performance, Kennedy simply said, "I don't think so" (quoted by "News of the Week," 1960, E1).

KENNEDY AND CATHOLICISM

In 1960, the nation had never had a president who was also a Catholic. One other Catholic candidate, Al Smith in 1928, had run, but not won the election. As Young (2015) wrote, Kennedy "faced steady anti-Catholic bigotry and constant questions about how his church's teachings would affect his presidency" (50). That belief was so strong that the Kennedy campaign felt that it was essential for the candidate to address this concern directly himself (Carty, 2004). As Menendez (2011) noted, "It was apparent to Senator Kennedy and his staff that he had to make a dramatic declaration of independence from his church's political involvement" (26).

The venue chosen for Kennedy's speech was the annual meeting of the Greater Houston Ministerial Association on September 12, 1960. There Kennedy would face a hostile audience of more than a thousand conservative ministers and religious laymen. Newman (2009) noted that Kennedy used the speech to address "issues regarding religion as a personal and private matter instead of a campaign issue" (691). Massa (1997) went further, arguing that the speech emphasized "the delineation of the role of religion in American politics" while also representing "the coming of age of American Catholicism" (307). Carty (2004) agreed with Massa, but also argued that Kennedy's success in the election was a sign of the nation evolving from its Protestant roots and into a nation that took a more pluralistic view of religion in general. Casey (2009) went further, arguing that the best way to describe the 1960 campaign was to say that it was about "The making of a Catholic president" (4).

In terms of the campaign, however, there appears little doubt that the speech was successful in easing concerns about how Kennedy's religious faith might influence his decisions as president. Even though it probably did not satisfy all of the fundamentalist Christians in the immediate audience, media coverage of the speech did mollify the fears of many in the electorate. As Strober and Strober (2015) noted, as a result of the speech and the question-and-answer period that followed, "Kennedy was finally able to defuse the religious issue" (38).

Kennedy eventually won the election and the speech in Houston was considered a crucial component of the campaign. Still, the actual importance of the speech may have been overrated. Menendez (2011) argued that Kennedy lost more votes because he was Catholic than he gained from the speech; instead, he further argued, Kennedy successfully put together coalitions of other voters to offset those losses. Still, the speech may have at least muted some of the religious opposition that Kennedy faced. And Schlesinger (2002) believed the speech had a positive impact on both Kennedy and the campaign, arguing that, as a result, "Kennedy himself was beginning to hit his stride" (68).

Further, the long-term impact of the speech may have been bigger. The election was, after all, the first time in a presidential campaign when a candidate reached out to the evangelical voters in the electorate. Newman (2009) argued that it was the beginning of "candidates who promoted their own faith, religious figures, and their goal of increasing the presence of religion in public life" (691). Thus, ironically, the ultimate impact of Kennedy's speech may have been just the opposite of what he was trying to achieve in the 1960 election. His goal was to attempt to remove religious faith as an element of the decision-making process for voters. But, by overtly acknowledging that his personal religious faith was an issue that needed to be addressed, he set the stage for religion to become a divisive factor in future elections.

THE DIRTY TRICKS OF DICK TUCK

Dick Tuck seemed to have a personal vendetta against Richard Nixon. Much of his political career was devoted to creating problems for the Nixon campaign. He was so effective that Miller (2004) later described Tuck as "the 20th century's premier political prankster" (34). Tuck did some of his most effective work during the 1960 presidential election.

Tuck viewed his role as that of political prankster; his pranks were well planned, disruptive, and creative for a great deal of internal problems of the Nixon campaign. Tuck started by arranging to get a paid position to do advance work for the Nixon campaign in California. One of his most famous tricks was working with Nixon on a whistle-stop campaign. The plan was simple. The campaign would lease a train that would travel from city to city. At each train station, Nixon would speak to a waiting crowd, using the caboose as his platform. When the speech was completed, the train would move to the next community and the process would be repeated. Tuck, however, ensured that the plan wouldn't work. He arranged to have two sets of clothing while traveling with the entourage, but he would change into clothing appropriate for a railroad worker once the train was stopped. Dressed like that, he would signal the engineer to start the train moving toward the next town while

Nixon was still speaking. The result was that Nixon's speech would be interrupted, time after time, as the train took off, carrying him away from the audience waiting to hear him.

Tuck's other famous prank occurred during a Nixon event in the Chinatown area of San Francisco. Tuck, as the advance person for the event, planned all aspects from signage to the menu at the final banquet for the day. He started with the signs that were scattered around Chinatown. Most, of course, were supposed to tout Nixon as a candidate. Instead, they included a number of attacks against Nixon, using Chinese characters that Nixon could not read (Stone & Colapietro, 2014). The crowning blow, however, came at the banquet. The meal itself went well, but every attendee received a fortune cookie that read, "Vote for Kennedy" (Powell & Cowart, 2010).

Tuck even got involved in the debate. After Nixon's poor performance in the first debate, as the candidate exited the studio, a woman outside loudly told him, "That's all right. You'll do better next time." The news coverage resulting from that exchange went national, but it wasn't a random remark. The woman had been hired by Tuck to embarrass Nixon (Thomas, 2015).

In retrospect, such antics seem somewhat humorous. But the Nixon campaign certainly didn't treat them that way. Instead, when Nixon returned to politics in 1968, he created a special group of campaign workers to play similar tricks on his Democratic opponents. Those workers had only a minor impact on the 1968 election. But they reached their most effective during the 1972 campaign, working under the unofficial title of "The Plumbers." In essence, the antics of Dick Tuck in 1960 became the justification for Nixon's dirty tricks in 1972, including the break-in of the Democratic headquarters in the Watergate building.

STEALING VOTES IN ILLINOIS

The final outcome of the 1960 election was so close that any number of factors could have made a difference in the election. The one that was particularly important, though, was the final vote numbers from the state of Illinois. Illinois was one of six states that were key to Kennedy's electoral strategy, with the others being New York, Pennsylvania, Michigan, Ohio, and California (Rorabaugh, 2009). Kennedy was declared the winner of Illinois by only about 8,000 votes. While "most of the media had declared [Kennedy] the winner" the night of the election (179), the actual vote count continued for weeks before being completed in December. As Donaldson (2007) noted, "the results were so close that the outcome is still questioned" (133). Still, that outcome was enough to get the state's electoral votes and give the Democrat the win (Schulman, 2013).

The catch? Nixon may have actually gotten the most votes from the state. The problem focused on voting irregularities in Chicago, the city that put Kennedy over the top for the state. Those irregularities were known to exist soon after the official results were announced (Mazo & Hess, 1968). Further, Kennedy also won Texas by a small margin; a shift in the votes from the two states combined would have been enough to give Nixon the win in the Electoral College (Matthews, 1996). In addition, the information about the irregularities in Illinois came to light so quickly that Nixon would have been well within his rights to contest the election. The shenanigans were attributed to the political machine of Chicago mayor Richard Daley, who had an almost iron-clad grip on political activities in the city. To his credit, Nixon chose not to challenge the results, arguing that a protracted legal fight over the outcome of the election would not be good for the nation. Still, it left him with a sour taste about politics in the state, one that he would carry with him for years.

Subsequent research on stealing elections has produced mixed results. Christensen and Colvin (2005) reported that Democrats were more likely to benefit from election irregularities, a finding that supports the assumptions of the 1960 election. However, Fund (2008) disagreed, arguing that Republicans were more frequently the beneficiaries of voter fraud. However, even Fund argued that "the electoral fraud in Richard Daley's Chicago . . . may have handed Illinois to John F. Kennedy" (9). Similarly, Stone and Colapietro (2014) argued that "voter irregularities . . . probably cheated Nixon out of his come-from-behind victory" (22).

Not everyone agrees. Kennedy ally Arthur Schlesinger (2002) labeled the idea of Kennedy stealing the election as "a recurrent myth" (xi). Schlesinger credits the win in Illinois to Kennedy's ability to attract black voters in Chicago. Regardless, if it was a myth, it was one that Nixon believed. And that belief colored many of his actions in the 1968 and 1972 elections.

CONCLUSIONS

The 1960 election was indeed an important one for the culture of blame and payback. Pietrusza (2010) argued that it essentially set the tone for both the 1964 and 1968 elections, resulting in the eventual election of Nixon in 1968. It was also a close one. Any number of factors in 1960 could have made a difference, including the debate performances of the candidates, Kennedy's speech on his Catholic faith, the pranks of Dick Tuck, or the voting irregularities in Illinois. Eventually, though, what really mattered for the future of American democracy is that 1960 served as a source of simmering tensions between the two parties. Kennedy's speech led to an increased emphasis on religion in American politics. The antics of Dick Tuck led to the justification for Nixon's dirty tricks in later years. In terms of attribution theory, the Republicans had a target to blame, and it was an easy case to justify. Further, the irregularities in Illinois gave the Republican a civics lesson on winning by stealing votes. Both set the stage for unethical campaigns in the future. In fact, Gifford (2009) argued that, despite the Democratic win, the 1960 election was the spark for the beginning of the conservative movement among Republicans.

REFERENCES

Benoit, W., & Harthcock, A. (1999). Functions of the great debates: Acclaims, attacks and defenses in the 1960 presidential debate. *Communication Monographs, 66,* 341–357.

Carty, T. A. (2004). *A Catholic in the White House?: Religion, politics, and John F. Kennedy's presidential campaign.* New York: Palgrave Macmillan.

Casey, S. (2009). *The making of a Catholic president: Kennedy vs. Nixon 1960.* New York: Oxford University Press.

Christensen, R., & Colvin, K. (2005). *Stealing elections on election night: A comparison of statistical evidence from Japan, Canada, and the United States.* Paper presented at the annual meeting of the American Political Science Association, Washington, DC.

Dailey, W. C., Hinck, E. A., & Hinck, S. S. (2007). *Politeness in presidential debates: Shaping political face in campaign debates from 1960 to 2004.* Mahwah, NJ: Rowman & Littlefield.

Donaldson, G. A. (2007). *The first modern campaign: Kennedy, Nixon and the election of 1960.* Lanham, MD: Rowman & Littlefield.

Fund, J. (2008). *Stealing elections: How voter fraud threatens our democracy.* New York: Encounter Books.

Gifford, L. J. (2009). *The center cannot hold: The 1960 presidential election and the rise of modern conservatism.* DeKalb: Northern Illinois University Press.

Halton, B. (2016). Presidential debates: Then and now. *Tennessee Bar Journal, 52*(4), 30–31.

Kraus, S. (2001). *The great debates: Kennedy vs. Nixon, 1960.* Bloomington: Indiana University Press.

Lehner, J. (2011). *Tension city: Inside the presidential debates, from Kennedy-Nixon to Obama-McCain.* New York: Random House.

Massa, M. S. (1997). A Catholic for president?: John F. Kennedy and the 'secular' theology of the Houston speech, 1960. *Journal of Church & State, 39*(2), 307–327.

Matthews, C. (1996). *Nixon and Kennedy: The rivalry that shaped postwar America.* New York: Touchstone.

Mazo, E., & Hess, S. (1968). *Nixon: A political portrait.* New York: Harper & Row.

Mehltretter Drury, S. A., & Herbeck, D. A. (2016). Remembering and re-creating the great debates of 1960: Presidential libraries as sites for political argumentation. *Communication Quarterly, 64,* 173–192.

Menendez, A. J. (2011). *The religious factor in the 1960 presidential election: An analysis of the Kennedy victory over anti-Catholic prejudice.* Jefferson, NC: McFarland.

Miller, T. (2004, August 30). Public life. *New Yorker, 80*(24), 34–35.

Minow, N. M., Martin, J. B., & Mitchell, L. M. (1973). *Presidential television.* New York: Basic.

Mlodinow, L. (2013). *Subliminal: How your unconscious mind rules your behavior.* New York: Vintage.

Newman, S. A. (2009). From John F. Kennedy's 1960 campaign speech to Christian supremacy: Religion in modern presidential politics. *New York Law School Law Review, 53*(3/4), 691–733.

The news of the week in review: Kennedy's week—from campaigning senator to president (1960, November 13). *Time,* E1.

Pietrusza, D. (2010). *1960—LBJ vs. JFK vs. Nixon: The epic campaign that forged three presidencies.* New York: Union Square Press.

Powell, L., & Cowart, J. (2012). *Political Campaign Communication: Inside and Out* (2nd Ed.). Boston: Pearson.

Rhea, D. M. (2012). There they go again: The use of humor in presidential debates 1960–2008. *Argumentation and Advocacy, 49(2),* 115–131.

Rorabaugh, W. J. (2009). *The real making of the president: Kennedy, Nixon, and the 1960 election.* Lawrence: University Press of Kansas.

Schlesinger, A. M. (2002). *A thousand days: John F. Kennedy in the White House.* New York: Houghton Mifflin.

Schneider, W. (2000, October 7). The 1960 debates' long shadow. *National Journal, 32(41),* 3210.

Schulman, M. (2013). *A history of American presidential elections: From George Washington to Barack Obama.* New Rochelle, NY: MultiEducator.

Self, J. W. (2005). The first debate over the debates: How Kennedy and Nixon negotiated the 1960 presidential debates. *Presidential Studies Quarterly, 35,* 361–375.

Stanton, F. (2000, September 25). The first debate over presidential debates. *Newsweek, 136(13),* 11.

Stone, R., & Colapietro, M. (2014). *Nixon's secrets: The rise, fall, and untold truth about the president, Watergate, and the pardon.* New York: Skyhorse Publishing.

Strober, D. H., & Strober, G. S. (2015). *The Kennedy presidency: An oral history of the era.* New York: HarperCollins.

Thomas, E. (2015). *Being Nixon: A man divided.* New York: Random House.

Wedley, K. (2010). How the Nixon–Kennedy debate changed the world. *Time.*

White, T. H. (2009). *The making of the president 1960.* New York: HarperCollins.

Young, N. J. (2015). *We gather together: The religious right and the problem of interfaith politics.* New York: Oxford University Press.

THREE

1964: Goldwater and the Solid South

The southern states had traditionally voted as a group for Democratic candidates for more than half of the decade, but that all changed in 1964. The year of 1963 was dominated with civil rights demonstrations across the South, with some events turning deadly. Three civil rights workers disappeared in Philadelphia, Mississippi; their bodies were later found buried in an earthen dam near the city. Viola Liuzzo was shot and killed by members of the Ku Klux Klan in Lowndes County, Alabama, while transporting demonstrators who were participating in the Selma march to Montgomery. Public outrage at such killings led to the passage of the Civil Rights Act in 1964, a piece of legislation heavily pushed and signed into law by President Lyndon B. Johnson.

While many of the voters knew little about LBJ prior to his ascension to the presidency, Johnson quickly and successfully associated himself with Kennedy and his popularity. As a result, Johnson easily won the Democratic nomination for president. His only opposition came from Alabama Governor George Wallace, who performed well in primaries in Maryland, Indiana, and Wisconsin (Carter, 2000; Frady, 2009). The Republicans, meanwhile, nominated Arizona senator Barry Goldwater to run against the president.

In the general election Goldwater lost badly, but the Republican won most of the southern states as white segregationist in the South deserted the Democrats in favor of the Republicans. It was the beginning of a reversal of the solid South, with Republicans' flair for seizing white voters who despised the Civil Rights Act and what it said about race relations. That trend would continue for most of the next fifty years, with only one exception, as Republicans used latent racist appeals to gain votes from the South and its heritage of Jim Crow laws.

Meanwhile, Democrats and Lyndon Johnson easily won the election. But Democratic control of the federal government also led to increased involvement by the United States in the Vietnam War. That polarized the nation and set the stage for future political fights over the war.

In terms of the Four Pillars Model of political campaigning (Kitchens & Powell, 2015), the dominant pillar for the 1964 election was fear. Johnson's campaign relied heavily on fear appeals in its attacks on Goldwater, particularly the image of Goldwater with his finger on the button controlling the nuclear bomb. An advertisement with a reputation as a fear appeal, i.e., the "daisy ad," only intensified since the election by tying Goldwater to the potential for nuclear war. The ad depicted a young girl picking petals off a daisy, with her count transforming into a countdown that led to the explosion of an atomic bomb. It is still considered one of the most controversial ads in the history of presidential campaigning (Mann, 2011). That approach had a major impact in the short haul, effectively painting Goldwater as representing an older, partisan position that did not fit the modern world. For the most part, though, the impact of Johnson's attack quickly evaporated once the election was over.

Not so for the Republican side. Goldwater's main argument was also fear, particularly in the South. His approach was to trigger the fears of white southerners that the civil rights movement would displace their political clout. That argument was also effective, with southern voters starting a transition of support from Democrats to the Republican Party. Even today, Republicans still use implied racism to keep white voters in the South on their side.

THE KENNEDY ASSASSINATION

President John F. Kennedy was assassinated in Dallas on November 22, 1963, less than a year before the 1964 election. The news gripped the nation. Many watched on live TV as the alleged assassin, Lee Harvey Oswald, was killed by Jack Ruby. They watched again as Vice President Lyndon Johnson was sworn into office, while Jacqueline Kennedy silently watched in her blood-stained dress. As White (1965) wrote, "It was, for Americans . . . a clap of alarm as startling as the memory of Pearl Harbor, so that forever they would ask one another—Where were you when you heard the news?" (6).

The assassination propelled Johnson into the White House, and he had only a few months to decide whether to run for his own term. After all, the New Hampshire primary was less than three months away. However, there seemed to be little doubt that he would be the natural choice for the Democratic nomination. To seriously consider someone else would have put a stain on the memory of John Kennedy. Johnson understood the importance of the public's feelings about the former president and frequently referred to him in his speeches. As Goodwin (1975) noted, "Johnson was able to act as both apprentice and caretaker—faithful agent of Kennedy's intentions and the healing leader of a stunned and baffled nation" (173).

But there were plenty of opportunities for the Republicans, at least in terms of the nomination. Nelson Rockefeller (Reich, 1996; Smith, 2014) represented the moderate wing of the party, hoping to sound more reasonable than the voices of the hard right. Leading the hard right move ment was Arizona Senator Barry Goldwater (Perlstein, 2001). The other candidates in the race included Governor William Scranton of Pennsylvania (Wolf, 1982), Senator Margaret Chase Smith of Maine (Schmidt, 1996; Sherman, 1999), Representative Walter Judd of Minnesota, Senator Hiram Fong from Hawaii (Faust, 2005), former governor Harold Stassen of Minnesota (Kirby, Dalin & Rothman, 2012), Representative John Byrnes of Wisconsin, and Ambassador Henry Cabot Lodge from Massachusetts (Estes, 2012). By the time of the Republican Convention, held at Daly City, California, only Scranton and Rockefeller were serious contenders, and Goldwater used his strict conservative principles to defeat both of them.

THE CIVIL RIGHTS MOVEMENT

In 1964, Johnson's support of civil rights legislation created a shift in the South toward the Republican Party after the Democrats had dominated since the Civil War. At the local level, contests were still won or lost in the Democratic primary; that pattern would continue for another two decades, with voters deciding local elections as Democrats but voting heavily Republican for most presidential candidates. As one Alabama voter told one of the authors during this period, "I don't have to vote for any Democrat to go anywhere except to Montgomery (the state capitol)." That attitude was common among white voters in the South during the 1964 election. As Donaldson (2016) wrote, "it was clear as civil rights became a more volatile issue that large numbers of southern whites would vote Republican under certain conditions" (4). In fact, the issue was not popular with all Republicans. Nelson Rockefeller "supported civil rights for African Americans" (25), and that seems to be one reason he did not garner the Republican nomination for president.

One of the most vivid images within the civil rights movement came in Birmingham, Alabama, in 1963. Commissioner of Public Safety Eugene "Bull" Connor turned loose dogs and turned on fire hoses to disrupt protesters, including children, in the city (Nunnelley, 1990; Brimmer, 2011). All of these events were captured on television cameras. As White wrote, "It was this that Martin Luther King, Jr., the Police Department of Birmingham, and American television were to provide in 1963: the visual demonstration of sin, vivid enough to arouse the conscience of the entire nation" (173–174).

As mentioned earlier, the most dramatic impact came in June 1964 with the disappearance of three civil rights workers in Neshoba County, Mississippi. The discovery of their bodies in an earthen dam in early August effectively galvanized the nation in support of the civil rights movement. Politically, the South quickly became isolated from the rest of the nation.

In the end, Johnson won by a landslide, despite losing the solid South. "In essence, the Democrats had become the party of civil rights" (Donaldson, 2016, 33). The Republicans, meanwhile, were identified with "an abandonment of civil rights and an acceptance of racism" (38). Those would turn out to be designations that still follow both parties today.

DEMOCRATS AND THE SOLID SOUTH

In terms of national elections, the American South has been influenced by racial issues since before the Civil War. Once the postwar carpetbaggers had departed the former states of the Confederacy, the South had essentially been a one-party state for Democrats. Voters in those states stood solidly behind the Democratic Party, primarily as a protest to the abolition of slavery enacted by Republican president Abraham Lincoln. Local elections were decided in local Democratic primaries, with no Republicans having real chances of winning, up through the 1960s.

Even Franklin Roosevelt, arguably the nation's most liberal president when he was first elected in 1932, received strong votes from the otherwise conservative South. Even efforts by the Wendell Willkie campaign to portray Roosevelt as friendly with blacks was ineffective at breaking the pro-Democrat bias in the South (Goodwin, 1995). After all, Roosevelt was a Democrat, and not one of those hated Republicans. That was enough for him to get their votes.

That all changed in 1964. With Johnson providing strong support for blacks in the South, white voters in the area opted for Goldwater. Johnson, meanwhile, did well in most other regions but had trouble in the South. As Williams (2013) noted, when Johnson tried to campaign in the South, he "had to face angry southerners" who were upset with his civil rights positions (248). In the end, it didn't matter much. Goldwater won five Deep South states in the election—Alabama, Georgia, Mississippi, Louisiana, and South Carolina—but Johnson won the nation. Since then, the Republican stranglehold on the South has merely intensified (Scher, 1997; Black & Black, 2003). As Black and Black wrote, "the southern activists who were inspired by Goldwater made plain their opposition to federal intervention on civil rights" (28). From a long-term perspective, this was a strategic mistake, as some Republican presidential candidates have now recognized. As Black and Black added, Republicans "foolishly wrote off black southerners at the very time when black participation was dramatically increasing" (138).

COORDINATED NEGATIVE CAMPAIGNS

Part of the campaign by Republicans to create a reversal of the solid South was a coordinated negative campaign against Lyndon Johnson. The idea was to give voters, particularly those in the South, a reason to vote against Johnson based on factors other than the civil rights movement. This campaign would be a forerunner of future negative campaigns. Similar to organized negative campaigns that would come later, there was no attempt in this effort to persuade voters to support Goldwater. Instead, the entire effort was to form a negative opinion of Johnson, under the assumption that a successful campaign would lead those voters to support Goldwater as the alternative.

Further, this campaign relied on heavily documented material. Most of the attacks were too detailed to present in 30-second ads. Instead, the primary medium used was that of paperback books. Even though most voters probably never read the books, they were widely distributed in the hopes that enough people would read them and pass along the negative information in them to their friends and neighbors.

Two books were key to the campaign, and both relied on fear appeals. The first, *A Texan Looks at Lyndon* (Haley, 1964), was a hatchet job on LBJ's record in Texas politics. The book's subtitle captured its theme: "A study in illegitimate power." The book looked back at Johnson's career, beginning with his 1948 Senate race. It delved heavily into irregularities in that race, raising questions (probably legitimate) about whether Johnson honestly won that election. After moving on to Johnson's record in the U.S. Senate, the book relied heavily on excerpts from the *Congressional Record* (some placed in the record by Johnson's enemies).

The second book was an ultra-conservative book, *None Dare Call It Treason* (Stormer, 1964), that promoted the political ideology of the John Birch Society. The book was published by Liberty Bell Press, a publishing unit formed by the author for the purpose of printing his own ideas. In a sign of future attacks, the author was a minister and religious conservative who was a member of the Republican Party. This book relied heavily on information from the Birchers as the basis of most of its text, but it was also supplemented with material from the *Congressional Record*. The thesis of the book was simple: when treason becomes a basic activity within the highest office of the nation (the Presidency), no critics have the courage to call it treason. As a result, Stormer argued that the U.S. was losing the Cold War because the President would not aggressively face the threat that came from the USSR.

The ultimate goal of the books was to give voters a reason to vote against Lyndon Johnson for reasons other than his support of civil rights. That way, voters could justify their opposition to Johnson on the basis of other issues, without admitting to themselves that they were racists who disliked him because he supported black voting rights. The books were such a silent part of the Goldwater campaign that many books on the election don't even mention them. Those that do are rarely complimentary. Middendorf (2006) described *None Dare Call It Treason* as written by a man who "found a Communist under every bed" (150) while describing the other book as depicting LBJ "as a compulsive wheeler-dealer" (150). Johnson (2009) simply described both as "right-wing hate literature" (230).

TELEVISION ADVERTISEMENTS

During the 1960 election, candidates and consultants tried to understand the power of television and what it could accomplish. By 1964, they had figured out the importance of television ads. In fact, one distinguishing characteristic of the 1964 election was its extensive use of television ads. It was the first presidential election to be dominated by this form of campaign communication. The ads were long by modern standards—a full 60 seconds instead of the standard 30-second commercials used by today's campaigns (Johnson, 2009). The use of television also expanded heavily into TV news as well. As Johnson wrote, "The expansion of the national media and the development of television news provided new avenues for reporters to cover politics and for politicians to reach the masses" (21).

The most famous ad of the campaign, and arguably the most famous political ad ever, was a single spot by the Johnson campaign that became popularly known as the "Daisy ad." The commercial depicted a young girl in a field, plucking petals off a daisy while trying to count from one to ten. As she approaches ten, a male voice takes over with a countdown to zero, followed by a nuclear explosion and a mushroom cloud. That was followed by the voice of Lyndon Johnson saying, "These are the stakes . . . ." The idea was to create doubts about putting the nuclear button in the hands of an arch-conservative such as Barry Goldwater. The ads final slogan was, "The stakes are too high for you to stay home." The ad triggered so many complaints to local stations, mostly by people upset with the jarring dichotomy of the little girl and the nuclear explosion, that the Johnson campaign immediately pulled it from the airways (Donaldson, 2016). Even today, the ad is considered one of the strongest fear appeals ever used in American politics (Healy & Kaplan, 2016). Further, the Johnson campaign continued with the same theme in subsequent ads, although with less disturbing visuals. In fact, the ad (coupled with the negative campaigning by Republicans mentioned above) is one reason that Milton (2016) considers the 1964 election to be one of the ten most negative campaigns in the history of presidential campaigning. He also considered the ad to be "the most effective presidential attack ad ever" (90). Similarly, Cummings (2007) called it "the most famous and effective campaign ad of all time" (225). Further, the Daisy ad was merely part of the campaign against Goldwater. As Dallek (2004) wrote, "Johnson's assault on Goldwater was a masterpiece of both covert and overt negative campaigning" (184). But the hallmark of that campaign remains the Daisy ad. As Updegrove (2012) noted, "Though it was shown only once, the commercial's message hit home, ushering in the era of negative television advertising that has flourished ever since" (127).

CONCLUSIONS

Johnson easily won the election, getting more than 60 percent of the popular vote. He did even better in the electoral college, winning by a margin of 486-to-52 while losing only five states in the South and Goldwater's home state of Arizona. Johnson even won the state of Alaska, the only time in its history that the state has voted for a Democratic presidential candidate. The results effectively sealed civil rights as a major issue for the nation and established that the Johnson administration was distinct from that of Kennedy. As Goodwin (1975) wrote, "The election of 1964 had given an independent legacy to his Presidency, his own ambitions and intentions detached from any responsibility for another's legacy" (213).

Meanwhile, the racial split in American politics also resulted in a split in partisanship. In fact, Perlstein (2001) traces the modern partisan division back to the 1964 election, blaming most of the problem at that time on the Goldwater campaign.

Goldwater obviously did not win, but his ideology was continued and became successful in 1980 when Ronald Reagan finally took that conservative mantle to victory. But the seeds of the success were first planted in 1964. Thus Johnson (2009) wrote, "The transformation of the Republican Party into a more ideologically cohesive, conservative political organization traces its roots to the 1964 primary season, which witnessed the last time an ideological moderate . . . had a legitimate chance of capturing the nomination" (11). Middendorf (2006) also traces the modern conservative movement back to the Goldwater campaign, even though he describes the campaign itself as "a glorious disaster" (1). And some pundits particularly point to the way in which Goldwater's team orchestrated the Republican convention that year. Reagan gave a speech in support of Goldwater in October "that has repeatedly been mistaken as the keynote speech at the Republican convention" (Skipper, 2016, 180), although the convention had occurred three months earlier.

REFERENCES

Black, E., & Black, M. (2003). *The rise of southern Republicans.* Boston: Belknap.

Brimmer, L. D. (2011). *Black and white: The confrontation between Reverend Fred L. Shuttlesworth and Eugene "Bull" Connor.* Boyd's Mill, PA: Calkins Creek.

Carter, D. T. (1995). *The politics of rage: George Wallace, the origins of the new conservatism, and the transformation of American politics.* New York: Simon and Schuster.

Cummings, J. (2007). *Anything for a vote: Cheap shots and October surprises in U.S. presidential campaigns.* Philadelphia: Quirk Books.

Dallek, R. (2004). *Lyndon B. Johnson: Portrait of a president.* New York: Oxford University Press.

Donaldson, G. A. (2016). *Liberalism's last hurrah: The presidential campaign of 1964.* New York: Skyhorse Publishing.

Estes, G. T. (2012). *Failed leadership of Ambassador Henry Cabot Lodge Jr.: A missed opportunity for peace in South Vietnam.* Auckland, New Zealand: BiblioScholar.

Faust, D. (2005). *Hiram Fong: Hawaii's first senator.* New York: Houghton Mifflin.

Frady, M. (2009). *Wallace: The classic portrait of Alabama Governor George Wallace.* New York: Random House.

Goodwin, D. K. (1975). *Lyndon Johnson and the American dream.* New York: Harper & Row.

Goodwin, D. K. (1995). *No ordinary time: Franklin and Eleanor Roosevelt: The home front in World War II.* New York: Simon & Schuster.

Haley, J. E. (1964). *A Texan looks at Lyndon. A study in illegitimate power.* Canyon, TX: Palo Duro Press.

Healy, P., & Kaplan, T. (2016, June 15). Old political tactic is required: Exploiting fear, not easing it. *New York Times,* A1, A16.

Johnson, R. D. (2009). *All the way with LBJ: The 1964 presidential election.* New York: Cambridge University Press.

Kirby, A., Dalin, D. G., & Rothman, J. F. (2012). *Harold E. Stassen: The life and perennial candidacy of the progressive Republican.* Jefferson, NC: McFarland.

Kitchens, J. T., & Powell, L. (2015). *The four pillars of politics: Why some candidates don't win and others can't lead.* Lanham, MD: Lexington.

Mann, R. (2011). *Daisy petals and mushroom clouds: LBJ, Goldwater, and the ad that changed politics.* Baton Rouge: Louisiana University Press.

Middendorf, J. W., II (2006). *A glorious disaster: Barry Goldwater's presidential campaign and the origins of the conservative movement.* New York: Basic Books.

Milton, G. W., Jr. (2016). *Nasty politics: The 10 most negative presidential campaigns in U.S. history.* North Charleston, SC: CreateSpace.

Nunnelley, W. (1990). *Bull Connor.* Tuscaloosa: University of Alabama Press.

Perlstein, R. (2001). *Before the storm: Barry Goldwater and the unmaking of the American consensus.* New York: Hill and Wang.

Reich, C. (1996). *The life of Nelson A. Rockefeller.* New York: Doubleday.

Schmidt, L. (1996). *Margaret Chase Smith: Beyond convention.* Orono: University of Maine Press.

Scher, R. K. (1997). *Politics in the new South: Republicanism, race and leadership in the 20th century.* Oxford, UK: Routledge.

Sherman, J. (1999). *No place for a woman: A life of Senator Margaret Chase Smith.* New Brunswick, NJ: Rutgers University Press.

Skipper, J. C. (2016). *The 1964 Republican Convention: Barry Goldwater and the beginning of the conservative movement.* Jefferson, NC: McFarland.

Smith, R. N. (2014). *On his own terms: A life of Nelson A. Rockefeller.* New York: Random House.

Stormer, J. (1964). *None dare call it treason.* Florissant, MO: Liberty Bell Press.

Updegrove, M. K. (2012). *Indomitable will: LBJ in the presidency.* New York: Crown.

White, T. H. (1965). *The making of the president 1964.* New York: Atheneum.

Williams, J. (2013). *Eyes on the prize: America's civil rights years, 1954–1965*. New York: Penguin.

Wolf, G. D. (1982). *William Warren Scranton: Pennsylvania statesman*. University Park: Pennsylvania State University Press.

FOUR

1968: The Rise and Fall of Republican Conservatism, Part I

During LBJ's full term in office, one of his major projects was the "War on Poverty." For conservatives, Democrat and Republican, Johnson's "war" presented problems of one sort or another. In both parties, many felt that the federal government was extending FDR's New Deal. Roosevelt had inaugurated Social Security and provided government jobs for many across the country. But FDR's plan was during the Great Depression. Southern Democrats saw Johnson's domestic program as a giveaway, primarily to African Americans. In fact, most of the benefits went to poor whites. In either case, these programs pushed the welfare state forward. Though the issue of the national debt had not been significant at the time, the debt began creeping up. Finally, the notion of big government versus small government was a concern of LBJ's opponents. The "toy" in this case was consumerism. Middle-class citizens complained of the welfare system and especially of low-income individuals using food stamps to purchase food. By using those stamps in grocery stores, it made the abstract concept of welfare a concrete, daily overt consideration. Opposition to LBJ was about both foreign and domestic policy.

Eventually, Johnson chose not to run for re-election. That led to a wide-open field in which the contenders included Robert Kennedy. Kennedy was actually the leading contender until his campaign was cut short by an assassin's bullet. Meanwhile, anti-war demonstrations continued through the Democratic Convention in Chicago. Hubert Humphrey ended up with the nomination, but he faced an uphill battle in his quest for the White House. The Republicans, meanwhile, settled on Richard Nixon who won the nomination in a comeback effort after losing to JFK in 1960.

The major pillars of the election were fear and national narcissism, based on the Vietnam War and the extent to which individuals supported or opposed the U.S. involvement in Southeast Asia. Families had a distinct fear of seeing their young men leaving to fight a war that many did not fully understand and the constant fear that those young men might not return home.

THE WAR ON POVERTY

Domestically, one of the most controversial components of Johnson's "War on Poverty" was the development of community action agencies. These agencies were administered locally, using various federal programs to carry out their missions. Among those programs was Head Start, an educational system devised to provide access and meals to underprivileged students before they enter kindergarten. Parents had to apply for their children to be admitted. Many in the middle class felt that minority children were given seats in these schools at the expense of lower-income whites. Another component of the system was the hiring of indigenous workers to manage the programs (Andre'L & Kaplan, 1968; Naples, 2014). Unfortunately, there was little training for these managers. Many of them would have been unqualified in most contexts. These jobs, which were relatively high paying, were frequently seen as welfare for minorities and career bureaucrats (Hickson III, 1971; Quadagno, 1996).

There were structural problems as well; the community action program's (CAP) local entities were required to report to a local board and to a federal district office. At the local level, many of those appointed were former local politicians who used their positions to continue their personal conflicts with those who were in elected offices as mayors, city council members, and county officials. At the district level, officials rarely visited the local offices, and when they did, they typically focused on complaints that had been filed against local community action groups. In relatively rural areas, the citizenry saw the programs as welfare for poor people, especially black people.

Throughout the south, integration was met with opposition and in several cases, violence, against white civil rights workers and blacks. Nevertheless, in July, LBJ signed the Civil Rights Act. The Supreme Court ruled that public accommodations should be available for all races. This meant that gasoline stations, restaurants, and hotels had to allow all races the use of their facilities. The Court based its decision on the commerce clause in the Constitution. Using the commerce clause had been a favorite mechanism for several changes that took place during FDR's administration. A sign had been used for decades in southern restaurants that read, "We reserve the right to refuse service to anyone." The Supreme Court now stated that restaurateurs did not have such a right.

Despite positive changes coming their way, many African Americans were still dissatisfied with their treatment by local and state governments. Bloody Sunday took place in Alabama the next year, when Martin Luther King, Jr. led hundreds of civil rights' supporters from Selma to Montgomery, Alabama. The march was stopped by state and local officials. One person was killed (Lee, 2002). They marched to support voting rights of black Americans, especially in the South. The same year, King won the Nobel Peace Prize. LBJ signed the Voting Rights Bill (Dierenfield, 2008). This was the final stake in the heart of segregationists who had tried to prevent blacks from voting. Given Johnson's State of the Union Address the next year, in which he initiated the Great Society program, LBJ's credibility among many white southerners appeared to disappear. Malcolm X was assassinated. The only black leader advocating separation was gone. King became the obvious leader of the civil rights movement.

Unfettered by the anti-civil rights actions, Johnson signed the Civil Rights Act, which eliminated segregation across the country. In the south, in particular, LBJ's actions not only enhanced the rights of black Americans, but also decreased the rights of its white citizens, as many felt that race relations involved a zero-sum game. Where separate seating had been practiced in movie theatres, no longer were blacks forced to sit in the balcony. No longer would there be separate doctors' waiting rooms for the two races. No longer would there be separate public water fountains. And, of course, no longer could states and communities send children to separate schools.

The changes escalated in the landscape of the south; the culture that had existed for more than 100 years was being challenged. Individuals were being challenged. States were being challenged. Local governments were being challenged.

THE WAR IN SOUTHEAST ASIA ESCALATES

The conflict in Vietnam continued. Robert McNamara, secretary of defense, issued the country's commitment economically and militarily to defeating the North Vietnamese. The contingent was increased to 21,000 troops early during the year. Later in the year, it was increased to 125,000. LBJ also indicated that he would increase the number of draftees from 17,000 to 35,000. Beginning with 3,500 combat troops, the number was steadily increasing. Many in America were beginning to believe that the country was entering the same quagmire that the French had been part of only a few years earlier. Opposition was led by young people, who were the likely draftees. Tens of thousands of opponents protested in front of the White House and the Washington Monument. The Gulf of Tonkin

Resolution passed, providing even more war powers to the president, while still not declaring war on North Vietnam.

Forty men at the University of California (Berkeley) burned their draft cards to protest the conflict. The SDS (Students for a Democratic Society) protested against the Vietnam War, bringing 25,000 to Washington. In 1968, the military strength in Vietnam reached its all-time high of more than 500,000 troops. The war was reaching the homes of virtually everyone in the country in one way or another. If someone in the family was not affected, certainly friends were involved as the draft increased, men were being killed, and many more were being wounded. Thus, in a "little skirmish" that only involved a few hundred advisors when Eisenhower was President, the conflict had turned into an all-out, though undeclared, war involving half a million soldiers on active duty in Vietnam as well as hundreds of thousands more who faced that potential fate.

According to the Selective Service System, conscriptions during Vietnam were 1,857,304 (Selective Service System, 2016). In comparison with the more than ten million during World War II, it was a relatively small number. But it was enough for almost every family to at least fear the possibility that a son or a nephew was a prospect.

OTHER ISSUES

Two important convictions took place. Jimmy Hoffa, the leader of the Teamsters Union, was convicted of jury tampering in a trial that took place in 1964. Hoffa had been connected to organized crime. Unions in general were opposed to the Republicans, who traditionally had sided with big business in their disputes. In most cases, the unions across the country voted in support of the Democrats. Second, Jack Ruby was convicted of murder in the death of Lee Harvey Oswald, the alleged assassin of President Kennedy. Ruby's shooting of Oswald was seen on live television across the country.

Later in the year, the Warren Commission Report was released to the public. The report was viewed as biased and incomplete. Part of the suspicion was that the entire report was not released, and to this day, has not been released. Conspiracy theories of all sorts emerged. They included ideas that the CIA or FBI had been part of the conspiracy as well as LBJ himself. Almost all of the theories suggested that Oswald was not the lone gunman. Others blamed the Cubans or the Russians.

In *Westberry versus Sanders*, the Supreme Court ruled that congressional districts must be approximately the same size in population. The intention was to prevent gerrymandering, the practice of creating unusual boundaries for districts to provide one party an advantage over another. In the states, the state legislative bodies generally approve such districts.

There have been several subsequent cases about the gerrymandering practice.

We should remember, too, that Vietnam was not the only foreign country with which we had a conflict. A naval intelligence ship, the U.S.S. *Pueblo* was captured by the North Koreans. The Cold War with the Soviet Union as well as with Communist China became more inflamed. The 11-month ordeal involved Lloyd Bucher, the captain of the *Pueblo*. The disagreement about whether the ship was in neutral waters continued. The Americans claimed that it was, and the North Koreans claimed that it was in their territory. LBJ was asleep when the actions occurred. American sailors were tied and blindfolded and threatened with bayonets. Eventually the sailors were released after the United States admitted that it was a spy ship. The incident, though, provided the first major, direct confrontation between the United States and the Soviet Union since the Cuban Missile Crisis.

Demonstrations took place against the war across the country and in other countries; by 1964 fewer than 300 had been killed or died in some other way. In 1965, the number was close to 2,000. In 1966, it was over 6,000. The numbers were growing exponentially. The largest number was in 1968, when close to 17,000 were killed. Whatever popularity for the war that had existed was decreasing quickly (Appy, 2016). Active and former soldiers were looked down upon by anti-war students. Whereas wearing a soldier's uniform in World War II was a prideful action, Vietnam had transformed wearing a uniform into a shameful action.

On the positive front in international politics, Khrushchev and Johnson signed an agreement to accumulate fewer nuclear weapon materials. Khrushchev was soon deposed and replaced by Brezhnev and Kosygin in Moscow.

Despite how things were going in the war, LBJ continued his civil rights' changes. Perhaps he felt that he could eliminate one of the protest groups' outrage at the federal government.

The United States and the Soviets continued their competition in space travel. Medicare and Medicaid were signed into law by LBJ. This increased the Social Security System that began with FDR. This meant a further escalation of the welfare state. Small government advocates of both parties were concerned that the country was increasing as a welfare state. LBJ signed the Immigration and Naturalization Act, which eliminated the quotas based on national origin.

1966–1967

In the state of Georgia, Julian Bond, a black civil rights leader was elected to the state legislature, but the legislature refused to seat him (Neary, 1971).

In short, the period between 1964 and 1968 showed a marked increase in divisions, especially class and racial divisions, within the country. If the civil rights movement and the anti-war movement were not enough for LBJ, the National Organization for Women (NOW) began protesting for the rights of women.

In January, Lester Maddox, an ardent segregationist, was elected governor of Georgia. Ronald Reagan, the former actor, was elected governor of California. The Tet Offensive began in South Vietnam with a number of surprise attacks including one at the U. S. Embassy in Saigon.

In March 1968, the country was shocked when LBJ announced on nationwide television that he would not seek re-election. This action followed a primary election against Eugene McCarthy, who ran on the single issue of bringing about peace in Vietnam. Johnson's victory over McCarthy was narrow. That primary was just 17 days prior to LBJ's speech. In the roughly five-minute speech, Johnson urged the country to stop the divisiveness both in terms of domestic and international causes. For many, it appeared that LBJ had been a failure in both domestic and foreign policy. As the years have passed, the country still views the policies regarding Vietnam as a negative period in American history. The civil rights legislation is now considered by most as a positive. LBJ's legacy, then, is a mixed bag. In politics, President Kennedy's brother, Robert, entered the Democratic primaries.

The next month, in April, Dr. Martin Luther King, Jr. was shot and killed in Memphis, Tennessee, fueling the divisions within the country (Peppers, 2003).

Robert Kennedy's entry into the presidential race was met with enthusiasm by many Democrats. Eugene McCarthy was viewed as a positive for the anti-war interests, but Kennedy had been attorney general. He was JFK's brother. His legal issues were helpful in LBJ's civil rights' legislation and enforcement. The hopeful dreams that Americans had when John Kennedy was elected had been thwarted by his assassination, but RFK's entry into the fray produced renewed hope. Although many initially did not like the idea of LBJ's replacing JFK, Johnson had made significant improvements in civil rights. McCarthy was viewed as weak in general, and there were fears that, with Johnson's decision not to run, the Democrats might lose the election. When King was killed, the dreams were lost once again. Now in the minds of many only RFK could recover the dream (Tye, 2016). On June 6, Kennedy won the Democratic primary in California. Soon thereafter, he was assassinated.

In the shadows was George C. Wallace, governor of Alabama (Carter, 1995). He had lost one gubernatorial election, primarily because he received support from the National Association for the Advancement of Colored People (NAACP). His opponent, a staunch segregationist John Patterson was supported by the Ku Klux Klan. Because of the loss, Wallace changed his position to favor segregation.

Wallace had stood in the schoolhouse door at the University of Alabama in 1963. He was confronted there by Deputy Attorney General Nicholas Katzenbach. The National Guard was called in to force Governor Wallace to remove himself. Three African Americans were allowed to register as students at the University of Alabama.

THE REPUBLICAN "SOUTHERN STRATEGY"

With Wallace running for the presidency as an independent, former vice president Richard Nixon devised what he called a "southern strategy." Based on previous elections in which the Dixiecrats separated from the Democrats and the southern votes were delivered to Goldwater in 1964, Nixon felt that most of the votes in the South were white votes because blacks were still less likely to register. It would be easy for the Republicans to win the southern states if only they did *not* support Johnson's numerous civil rights' actions. In essence, Nixon appealed to the southern segregationists. Of course, the Republicans would have to "out-southern" the rhetoric of George Wallace. The appeal would be a more sophisticated, passive racist approach.

Once Johnson decided not to run, the route to the White House appeared easier for Nixon, who had been defeated by Kennedy in the 1960 election, which was never challenged by Nixon. Nevertheless, Nixon felt he had been cheated out of the election. Nixon then lost an attempt to become governor of California. Many expected him to leave politics completely. He himself stated publicly that the press would no longer have to deal with him. To most people, this meant that Nixon was out of politics altogether. Now he was back.

His route to the presidency had become easier because Nelson Rockefeller had divorced and almost immediately remarried, which was scandalous to voters at the time. Other Republican potential candidates did not appear strong. Obviously, because of his monumental defeat in 1964, Goldwater would not be seriously considered. In the Democratic Party, McCarthy did not seem to have a strong appeal.

Although the southern segregationists still resented the Republicans because of Lincoln and the Civil War (100 years earlier), and the fact that most of the Reconstructionist, carpetbagging Yankees came from the Republican Party, the alternatives left for the South were only two. The hopes of Wallace gaining the Democratic nomination appeared negligible, though the South could vote for him as an independent. However, the success of third-party candidates in the United States had been extremely weak. Nixon figured that their alternative would be to vote with the Republicans, using the LBJ civil rights' legislation as the vehicle for victory. No one came outright and suggested that the Republican Party was supporting racism, but the implications were strong and continue to this day.

THE CONVENTIONS AND THE GENERAL ELECTION

In early August, at the Republican Convention in Miami Beach, Nixon won on the first ballot, defeating New York's Nelson Rockefeller and California's Ronald Reagan. Nixon chose Spiro T. Agnew, governor of Maryland, as his running mate.

The general lack of controversy at the Republican Convention would certainly not be a prelude to what happened at the Democratic Convention in Chicago. Eugene McCarthy had run against LBJ in the New Hampshire primary, and although he had done well, it appeared that his single issue of Vietnam might not be enough to win in the general election. When Johnson indicated that he would not run, Vice President Hubert Humphrey decided to run, despite not participating in the primaries (Solberg, 1984). He won delegates from states with caucuses, which were run by party regulars. McCarthy's followers attempted to add a peace plank to the party's platform. That move was defeated by about a 60–40 vote. Many believe that Chicago mayor Richard Daley and LBJ worked behind the scenes to see to it that the plank was defeated.

Robert Kennedy's assassination left his delegates uncommitted. Daley had intended for the convention to be a national showcase for the city. However, riots broke out, comprised mostly of young, anti-war protesters and supporters of McCarthy. In reality, though, it was more than that. Many of the observers inside and outside saw the convention as a conflict between the traditional establishment Democrats of Johnson, Humphrey, and Daley and the anti-war groups of McCarthy and Kennedy. And there was more. It was also a place for people to make decisions whether they supported the Johnson wing of the party or the Kennedy wing.

Security guards for the convention grabbed CBS correspondent Dan Rather and roughed him up. Rather had been on the floor of the convention reporting on the conflicts that were taking place. Walter Cronkite, the CBS news anchor, referred to the security guards as thugs. Cronkite was considered one of the most credible sources in the country at the time. The convention left Rather perceived as liberal more than objective. This view would hold to Rather for many years as he would eventually replace Cronkite as the anchor of the *CBS Evening News*.

Daley, resenting the protesters, said that these people would never take over his city. There were about 10,000 protesters and more than double that many policemen. Seven of the protesters were arrested and charged with conspiracy. They became known as the "Chicago Seven." When the cases went to court, Bobby Seale, a leader of the Black Panther Party, was also indicted to make the Chicago Eight (Feiffer & Hayden,

2006). While these protesters held some legitimate concerns, they were also making fun of the entire process. Led primarily by Abbie Hoffman and Jerry Ruben, among other things they threated to put LSD in Chicago's water supply. Television cameras were spending about as much time covering the protesters as they were covering what was going on in the convention.

Another leader of the protests was Tom Hayden, a leader of the Students for a Democratic Society (SDS). The protesters used the phrase, "Hell no, we won't go," but Hayden tried to get them to leave the park area across from the convention site. Daley ordered tear gas against the protesters, and many blamed the mayor and the Chicago police for causing the problems. The perspective on who was to blame depended in large measure on the age of the viewer. Seven of the eight were either acquitted or convicted on lesser charges, but the convictions were reversed on appeal.

The fact that the situation, inside and outside the convention, was constantly on television divided Americans who were Democrats. Chicago was seen as a militaristic version of Chicagoan Al Capone's gang. While the reputation did not remain for long, it was certainly there. Mayor Daley remained in office.

Nixon's southern strategy was both successful and unsuccessful. He was handicapped by George C. Wallace who ran on the American Independent Party ticket (Carter, 1995). Wallace took away southern states that would otherwise have gone for Nixon. But with Goldwater's taking the states in 1964 and Wallace in 1968, along with the Dixiecrats earlier, it certainly seemed that the Democrats had lost their "solid South." It was still the solid South but not for the Democrats.

It was Daley's actions in the 1960 election that many felt gave the election to John F. Kennedy. Daley was a political boss who was used to getting his way in his city. It is somewhat ironic that Chicago was the city where Nixon had lost the 1960 election. At the same time it was the actions of Daley and the Chicago police that helped Nixon win in 1968 (Royko, 1971). Many Democrats felt that Hubert Humphrey had "stolen" the nomination, and others felt that Humphrey had been unfairly bound to LBJ regarding the war. The Democratic Party was broken and it would need to be fixed by 1972. Nixon's election meant that he had been "vindicated" from the 1960 disaster, but he couldn't take credit for it. The Democrats had shot themselves in the foot.

In fact, Democrats may have been better off had they shot themselves in the foot. The two issues that had disrupted the nation for decades were now two separate, serious issues for the Democrats. The Vietnam War posed significant problems. It had become obvious that the number of people opposing the war was increasing by the day. Demonstrations were taking place all over the country. McCarthy's popularity and, to some extent, RFK's popularity were built on anti-war positions. Now one was gone and the other almost forgotten. Despite the fact that Eisenhower had initially sent "advisors" to Vietnam, it was LBJ who increased the numbers from a few to 100,000. It was LBJ who had increased the draft (Flynn, 1993). All of a sudden, middle class white men were being sent to Vietnam. Virtually every healthy, young man feared the worst—in a war that many thought could never be won. Ultimately, all of these actions affected voters in the more liberal, anti-war states.

Southerners were not as opposed to the war as the rest of the country, for at least two reasons. First, historically southerners have always "served" as a matter of obligation. Rarely do southerners oppose wars regardless. Second, for the most part, draft boards in the South were sending their finest black men to Southeast Asia, until the lottery took place. Southerners had a different problem. The opposition to LBJ's civil rights' legislation was beginning to affect their culture. George Wallace had taken away 45 southern electoral votes. Should Wallace run again, the likelihood was that he would be even more successful. But what had happened was that Nixon took Virginia, North Carolina, South Carolina, Tennessee, and Florida. The Republicans "southern strategy" was paying off. Nixon didn't even have to mention segregation after LBJ's actions in favor of civil rights. For segregationist southerners, if anyone was on their side, it was *not* the Democrats.

CONCLUSION

The 1968 election saw a continuation of the us-versus-them politics that emerged in 1964, further establishing a foundation for the culture of blame and payback. However, the Democrats came out of the 1968 election in disarray. Humphrey had run a remarkable campaign, considering how far behind he started after the Democratic convention and the fact that he made it a close election. Still, the overall image of the Democratic Party was one of disorganization. Further, the Democrats' loss in 1968 established a trend that would continue for more than two decades in which they would win only one presidential election.

Nixon won, but not impressively. In fact, the 1968 Nixon campaign became the basis of a popular book, *The Selling of the President,* which documented how Nixon's consultants worked to refurbish his image for television and with ads to ensure that he would win (McGinnis, 1969). The book became an early primer on consultants' impact on campaigns, while overlooking the fact that they nearly mishandled the candidate by starting with a big lead and barely holding on to victory. Regardless, the trend toward having consultants to help a candidate's image was now firmly established for future elections.

Meanwhile, the animosity between the two parties took another step forward. The Democrats took an electoral blow that followed them into the 1990s, while the Republicans felt they had established a pattern for winning national elections in the future. In particular, the Republican southern strategy was working and would continue to work in the future.

REFERENCES

Andre'L, D., & Kaplan, S. J. (1968). The myth of the indigenous community leader: A case study of managerial effectiveness within the "War on Poverty." *Academy of Management journal, 11*(1), 11–25.

Appy, C. G. (2016). *American reckoning: The Vietnam War and our national identity.* New York: Penguin.

Carter, D. T. (1995). *The politics of rage: George Wallace, the origins of the new conservatism, and the transformation of American politics.* New York: Simon & Schuster.

Dierenfield, B. J. (2008). *The civil rights movement.* New York: Routledge.

Feiffer, J., & Hayden, T. (2006). *Conspiracy in the streets: The extraordinary trial of the Chicago Eight.* New York: New Press.

Flynn, G. Q. (1993). *The draft.* Lawrence: University Press of Kansas.

Hickson, M. L. III (1971). *A systems analysis of communication adaptation in a community action agency* (Unpublished doctoral dissertation). Southern Illinois University, Carbondale, IL.

Lee, T. (2002). *Mobilizing public opinion: Black insurgency and racial attitudes in the civil rights era.* Chicago: University of Chicago Press.

McGinnis, J. (1969). *The selling of the president.* New York: Trident Press/Simon & Schuster.

Naples, N. A. (2014). *Grassroots warriors: Activist mothering, community work, and the war on poverty.* New York: Routledge.

Neary, J. (1971). *Julian Bond: Black rebel.* New York: William Morrow & Co.

Quadagno, J. (1996). *The color of welfare: How racism undermined the war on poverty.* Oxford: Oxford University Press.

Peppers, W. F. (2003). *An act of state: The execution of Martin Luther King.* Brooklyn, NY: Verso.

Royko, M. (1971). *Boss: Richard J. Daley of Chicago.* New York: E. P. Dutton.

Selective Service System (2016, April 19). Induction statistics. Taken from selectiveserviceus/military-draft/8induction.shtml. April 19, 2016.

Solberg, C. (1984). *Hubert Humphrey: A biography.* New York: W. W. Norton.

Tye, L. (2016). *Bobby Kennedy: The making of a liberal icon.* New York: Random House.

FIVE

1972: Nixon and the Plumbers

Saturday morning, June 17, 1972. The Nixon campaign was poised for re-election. The Democrats had not yet nominated anyone for president, but Nixon maintained his paranoia over losing the election to Kennedy in 1960. He did not want to take any chances this time. *Washington Post* police reporter Alfred Lewis reported in the Sunday paper that five suspects were arrested the previous morning at 2:30 for breaking into the Watergate Building, near the Kennedy Center on Virginia Avenue (Lewis, 1972). The culprits were found in the Democratic National Committee's office, specifically the office of National Chairman Lawrence O'Brien. The details, as many as there were, came from the accused burglars' appearances in court later that Saturday. The extent to which this break-in story was relevant to much of anything was certainly controversial, with Republicans suggesting there was not much to it and Democrats' seemingly blowing the incident out of proportion. Using Lewis's police reporter story as the basis, Ben Bradlee, the editor of the *Post*, assigned two reporters to investigate the alleged crime in more detail. As the story turns out, it is certainly ironic that this burglary occurred near the Kennedy Center.

Two days after the crime took place, Woodward and Bernstein added to the story (Woodward & Bernstein, 1972). They reported that one of the suspects, James McCord, was employed as security coordinator of the Nixon re-election organization. Former attorney general John Mitchell, now the head of the Republican Committee to Re-elect the President (CREEP), stated that McCord and others were hired to install the Republican National Committee's own security. Mitchell claimed that they were not authorized to engage in the activities for which they were accused. A spokesman for CREEP said that he did not know who hired McCord, but he said it was not Mitchell. The police, at the arrest, said that

bugging devices were found in O'Brien's office. The accused were referred to as "the Plumbers."

"The Plumbers" were given that name as a major part of their mission
to stop intelligence leaks, such as those delivered to the *New York Times*
by Daniel Ellsberg. The leaks, called *The Pentagon Papers* were published
in segments during the previous year by the *Times*. Weeks later, the entire
compilation of papers was published as a book. Ellsberg claimed that the
papers contained information that the American public needed to know
because much of it had never been reported in the media. Security-con-
scious Nixon was hardly criticized in the papers because the contents
were mostly about the Johnson administration's handling of the war in
Vietnam. The claims were that the war had been expanded into Laos and
Cambodia as well as North Vietnam.

Henry Kissinger, the national security advisor, persuaded Nixon that
the government needed to begin taking action to prevent these intelligence leaks to the public. While some of the Pentagon Papers were classified, most were relatively old in context. Kissinger's concern was that
the actions such as those of Ellsberg would be repeated. Thus, "the Plumbers" were created to stop the leaks.

NIXON'S CAMPAIGN AND HIS RECORD

Nixon's concern was as much about the election as national security.
Although his approval ratings were in the 30s, when compared with
potential Democratic candidate George McGovern, the polls showed Nixon ahead by more than 20 points in May. Despite the Watergate issue,
Nixon's numbers continued about the same through the election in November.

The break-in was a "hot topic" inside the Beltway, but outside of
Washington, most people were either unaware of it or thought it was
another dirty trick that the public had become accustomed to in election
campaigns. The *Post* was the only major paper that took Watergate seriously. Perhaps the lack of interest was because the *Times* had undergone
enough criticism about the Pentagon Papers, but also the *Times* required
more backup before publishing this kind of explosive material. Views
ranged from concerns about the Republican Party under Nixon's leadership to the idea that the Democrats set up the whole situation as part of
their own dirty tricks' repertoire. For many voters, it was simply politics
as usual.

In fact, Nixon probably had little to worry about. One of the leading
Democratic candidates, George Wallace (Alabama) had been shot and
seriously wounded while campaigning in Maryland just a month earlier.
Wallace was to live the remainder of his life in a wheelchair. His political
campaign for President in 1972 was over. Nixon was perhaps more con-

cerned about Wallace than other potential candidates, certainly peace candidate George McGovern. Wallace was popular among conservatives. There was a good chance that Wallace could carry the southern states if he were nominated. Despite Nixon's low popularity, most would have claimed that his record as president was good.

Earlier in the year, Nixon had made a historic trip to the People's Republic of China. The trip was seen as a significant attempt at improving relations with the world's most populous country. The meeting with Chairman Mao Tse-tung helped improve the president's image in foreign policy as Nixon was receiving accolades during this important election year. It was the first time in 25 years that there had been a hint of relations between the two countries.

Nixon had agreed to remove American troops from South Vietnam as part of a cease-fire. Nevertheless, the North Vietnamese walked out of the Paris Peace Talks because of continued American bombings in Southeast Asia. Meanwhile, the Soviets signed an agreement with Libya, allowing for increased communist presence in Africa. While Vietnam continued to be a hotbed of conflict, the conflict in Ireland was also heating up. Because of the number of Irish Americans living in the United States, the government at least officially stayed away from Irish politics.

Domestically, the women's movement was progressing. Congress passed the Equal Rights Amendment and sent it to the states for ratification. The Vietnam War had created a situation in which there was questioning about 18-year-olds being allowed to vote. A few states had been allowing 18-year-olds suffrage, but most had not. The 26th Amendment to the Constitution had passed in 1971, mostly based on the argument that if men could be drafted and die in Vietnam at age 18, they should also be allowed to vote.

In the previous year, Amtrak began providing passenger rail service between cities in the United States, especially in the eastern corridor.

Despite all of the positives surrounding the Nixon presidency, his approval ratings were consistently low. Even though he had been elected in 1968, the American people still did not like him. In large measure, as the years went on, his campaign promise to end the war in Vietnam had not been consummated. It seemed that the war had gone on and on; it had become the country's longest war. With the lottery in place for the draft, the deferments that many white, middle-class boys had received in the past had disappeared. More than half of the people disapproved of the war.

THE DEMOCRATS PREPARE FOR THE ELECTION

Among Democrats, Nixon's administration was not seen in such a positive light. He had not ended the war, as he had claimed he would do in the 1968 election. The Pentagon Papers certainly seemed to indicate that the United States' military efforts were much less successful than the administration and the Pentagon had claimed. The economy was not doing well, as was illustrated by Nixon's imposition of wage and price controls to slow down inflation. It is interesting to note that wage and price controls had never been imposed previously on a strictly economic argument. In many ways, the procedure was extremely liberal. Add to that Nixon's discussions with Mao, another liberal move, and it became clear that many conservative Republicans began viewing Nixon as sitting on the left side of moderation.

Nixon's handling of civil rights also came into play. Attempting to steer a moderate course on busing and affirmative action, Nixon was displeasing conservatives and liberals alike.

Because Humphrey had failed to win in 1968, there was no obvious choice for the Democrats. It was a time when there was a large field of candidates, although several probably had little chance of winning from the outset. Humphrey decided to run anyway, although he received a majority of votes only in West Virginia. Of the 14 candidates, only two received at least 20 percent of the vote in the first caucus in Iowa: George McGovern and Edmund Muskie. Muskie had been Humphrey's vice presidential nominee. McGovern was a senator from South Dakota, who was carrying the peace flag, formerly held by Eugene McCarthy.

Shirley Chisholm, who had been elected the first African American woman to the House of Representatives, ran for the nomination. Her numbers were generally low, but some have suggested that she paved the way for both Barack Obama and Hillary Clinton. Her campaign ended early, and she did not even get on the ballot in a number of states. Eugene McCarthy lost in Illinois, and it soon became obvious that his failed attempt in 1968 would not help him in 1972.

George C. Wallace, the governor of Alabama and previous independent candidate for president, did not start until after the New Hampshire primary. But a week after the New Hampshire primary, Wallace won in Florida, taking almost 42 percent of the vote. He took second place in Wisconsin and Indiana. Wallace won in Tennessee with 68 percent of the vote. In North Carolina he received a majority of votes.

On May 15, Wallace was shot. In the Maryland primary the next day, Wallace continued to poll the most votes. On that same day, he won Michigan with a majority. At that point, though, it was common knowledge that he could not serve with his physical incapacities.

The 1972 convention started on July 10, in Miami Beach, Florida.

Muskie and McGovern had been in a dead heat for the nomination. But Muskie was attacked in the Manchester, New Hampshire, newspaper, accused of using a drug and for verbally attacking Canadian-Americans. The first charge had come from a letter, which the paper published. Later, the paper attacked Muskie's wife for drinking and telling off-color jokes during the campaign. At a press conference held outside while it was snowing, Muskie defended his wife. During his defense some members of the media said that he was crying. Muskie later said that there were no tears, but rather there were snowflakes. In any case, all of these charges caused his demise in the campaign. With Muskie and Wallace out, George McGovern became the candidate. After the Watergate affair, the press learned that all of the attacks on Muskie were created by Nixon's anti-Democratic machine, possibly including some of the Plumbers.

McGovern chose Tom Eagleton of Missouri as his running mate. That pairing didn't last long. Various charges were made against Eagleton, including the accusation that Eagleton was seeing a psychiatrist for a depression disorder. McGovern then replaced Eagleton with Sargent Shriver, who had been an ambassador to France, but most notably was an in-law of the Kennedy family. McGovern's failure to vet Eagleton and his indecisiveness about dropping him from the ticket brought about new charges of McGovern's incompetence from the Republicans. In the case of Eagleton, there was just enough truth to the argument against him that the dirty tricksters had little to do. Much of what they did do was more exaggeration than plain untruths.

THE *POST* CONTINUES TO INVESTIGATE "THE PLUMBERS"

With the Democratic Convention just weeks away, Woodward and Bernstein continued their investigative reports. They found that a check for $25,000, intended for CREEP, had been deposited in one of the Plumbers' personal account. No one for the Re-election Committee could explain how the check got there (Woodward & Bernstein, 1972b). Hundred dollar bills that were withdrawn from a Boca Raton, Florida, bank were also in possession of some of the Plumbers. Altogether there was about $5,300 in cash. The banker said that the FBI had asked questions about these actions a couple of months earlier.

Nixon was much less concerned about the FBI than he should have been. J. Edgar Hoover, the only director, from the 1920s, died on May 2, 1972, just a few weeks before the Watergate break-in. Nixon and Hoover apparently got along well, but Nixon thought the FBI would be less competent under new director L. Patrick Gray, whom Nixon appointed to replace Hoover.

Woodward and Bernstein, in their August 9 report, also wrote that they had found a connection between at least two of the burglars and a consultant, E. Howard Hunt, Jr. One member of the CREEP organization, G. Gordon Liddy, was also associated with the burglars in June. Mitchell had stepped down from his CREEP position. Charles ("Chuck") Coulson, a counsel to the president in the White House, was "connected to the crime," according to a lawsuit that Lawrence O'Brien took to court.

On September 29, Woodward and Bernstein released another story about Watergate (Woodward & Bernstein, 1972c). They found that John Mitchell, when he was attorney general, had controlled a secret Republican fund intended for discovering negative information about the Democrats. Certainly, negative campaign tactics against the opposition had been used previously by both parties. This secret intelligence fund had balances of between $350,000 and $600,000. Mitchell had approved checks on the account. When called by *Post* reporters, Mitchell's response was that all of the charges had been denied and that Katharine Graham, the publisher of the *Post*, would be in serious trouble after the situation was over. He hung up the phone. Other top officials of the re-election group had been involved in the finances. By this time, the Woodward and Bernstein investigative strategy of "follow the money" was fully in operation.

On October 10, there was another report, this time based on information from the FBI. The *Post* reporters wrote that FBI agents had found that the break-in was only a small part of a subversive plan to politically destroy all of the leading Democratic candidates. They wrote that "Following members of Democratic candidates' families and assembling dossiers on their personal lives; forging letters and distributing them under the candidates' letterheads; leaking false and manufactured items to the press; throwing campaign schedules into disarray; seizing confidential campaign files; and investigating the lives of dozens of Democratic campaign workers" were all part of the group's actions (Woodward & Bernstein, 1972d). This is when the *Post* first reported that the "Canuck" letter had been forged, which is part of what led Muskie to end his campaign. Just a few days later, Nixon was re-elected in one of the largest landslides in American history.

THE ELECTION DOES NOT STOP *POST* REPORTERS

For Ben Bradlee, Woodward, and Bernstein, the story was not over simply because the election was. Lawrence Meyer, another *Post* reporter wrote about Liddy, McCord, and others being convicted in actions involving Watergate (Meyer, 1973). E. Howard Hunt pleaded guilty. John Sirica, the district judge, presided over the cases.

Following the money, the responsibility for these illegal activities going back as far as 1971, was moving higher and higher up the food chain. By May, H. R. Haldeman and John Ehrlichman, two of Nixon's top aides in the White House, had resigned, as did Attorney General Richard Kleindienst, who had replaced Mitchell just months before. Kleindienst admitted that he had charged the FBI with investigating the break-in and other possible criminal activities associated with it. Kleindienst had been the only member of the administration who had been paying more attention to doing his job than in covering up the past. At this point, there is little doubt that Nixon's concerns were becoming more and more serious. Nixon fired his counsel, John Dean, whom Nixon had ordered to investigate the break-in (Stern & Johnson, 1973).

The designated attorney general, Eliot Richardson, named Archibald Cox, a former solicitor general, as a special prosecutor, provided the Senate approved. The move, at least in part, was to hopefully assure the public that no one else was involved. Cox was a Democrat who had worked for John Kennedy. There would be no appearance of Republican bias. The Democrats were not satisfied that Cox would be working for Nixon's Justice Department. They had no objection to Cox having the position, but they wanted the prosecutor to be independent.

A seven-member Senate investigation committee began in May 1973. That investigation would continue for 13 months. Sam Ervin (D-NC) was the chairman, and Howard Baker (R-TN) was the ranking member. At this juncture, at least three investigations were going on. The Senate committee, the FBI, and the special prosecutor. Presumably, the special prosecutor was working with the FBI. The committee hearings were carried live on the three major television networks, ABC, CBS, and NBC. Public radio also carried the hearings.

On June 3, 1973, Bernstein and Woodward answered the question about John Dean's involvement. In a news story, they reported (Bernstein & Woodward, 1973) that Dean said he would testify before the Watergate committee, whether or not he was granted immunity. Dean said that Nixon knew of the cover-up efforts regarding the Watergate burglary and related issues. The reporters' "source" said that Dean would say that Haldeman, Ehrlichman, and Nixon were in the same room when plans for the cover-up were created. The White House, Haldeman, and Ehrlichman claimed that it was Dean who was behind the cover-up. Dean said that more than $400,000 had been spent in hush money and that Nixon was aware of it. Dean said that, in a phone call with Nixon, he told the president that it would take another million dollars to maintain the cover-up.

In a related story on the same day, Woodward and Bernstein (1973), reported that Cox's investigations found that some of the Plumbers had been involved in the break-in of Daniel Ellsburg's psychiatrist's office. The plans for that break-in were reported to John Ehrlichman in a letter found by Cox's committee.

In July, the Senate committee was moving rapidly. Alexander Butterfield, who had worked in the White House (now with the Federal Aviation Administration), testified that Nixon had been recording conversations since 1971, presumably for historical purposes. Because the recordings were so pervasive and few people knew about them, Butterfield suggested that the tapes would prove "once and for all" whether Nixon knew about the cover-up (Meyer, 1973b). Only five days after Butterfield's revelation, Nixon had the recording system dismantled.

On October 20, Nixon refused to turn over any tapes to either the Senate committee or the special prosecutor. Nixon ordered Elliot Richardson to fire Cox, since the special prosecutor was technically working for the Justice Department. Richardson refused and resigned in the process. Nixon then ordered William Ruckelshaus to fire Cox and close the special prosecutor office. He also refused. The White House claimed that Ruckelshaus was fired; Ruckelshaus claimed that he resigned. Nixon then ordered Robert Bork, the next in line, to fire Cox and Bork complied, sending Cox a letter indicating he had been fired. But the district court ruled the firing illegal. The process continued as the offices of Richardson, Ruckelshaus, and Cox were closed by the White House. Nixon announced that the Justice Department would take over the special prosecutor's responsibilities (Kilpatrick, 1973). These events were known as the Saturday Night Massacre. Public opinion against Nixon was now quite strong—with thousands of messages sent to Congress and the White House.

Unrelated but not insignificant was the fact that Vice President Spiro Agnew had resigned from office ten days earlier. Agnew was charged in a number of bribery cases when he was governor of Maryland. Agnew was never accused of anything related to the Watergate affair. House Minority Leader Gerald Ford was approved as the new vice president.

Most of the issues over the next few weeks involved the tapes. Nixon finally released some. However, there was a gap of about 18 minutes of conversation between Nixon and Bob Haldeman. By this time, those defending Nixon had decreased significantly. District Judge Sirica ordered the tapes be made available to investigators. Eventually the White House released more than 1,200 pages of transcripts of taped conversations made inside the office and on the telephone.

Nixon still maintained "executive privilege" regarding some of the tapes, but the U. S. Supreme Court ruled that Nixon had to turn over additional tape recordings/transcripts. On July 27, 1974, three days after the Court ruling, written by Chief Justice Burger, there were massive calls for Nixon's impeachment, which began under the auspices of the House of Representatives. Nixon resigned August 9, 1974, and Gerald Ford became the 40th President of the United States. Less than a month later, Ford granted an unconditional pardon to Nixon. This action was a contributing cause of Ford's losing the election to Jimmy Carter, former governor of Georgia, in 1976.

THE COUNTRY'S DARKEST DAYS

With the exception of the American Civil War, the second term of Richard Nixon was arguably the worst time in the history of the country. What had begun as a relatively uncontroversial break-in at the Watergate Building had ended the careers not only of the plumbers, but also of several top aides in the White House. The reputations of Haldeman, Ehrlichman, Hunt, and Liddy were stained forever. Alexander Haig, who replaced Haldeman, maintained a place in politics. Robert Bork's relatively minor role in the fixing of Cox did not hurt him immediately, but it was one of those actions that would come back to haunt him much later when he was nominated as a Supreme Court justice.

Nixon had come close to rivaling Andrew Johnson on the list of unpopular American presidents, despite all that he had done in creating a relationship with China and creating the platform for ending the war in Vietnam. Anyone who was living at the time would say that what they remembered about Nixon was that he was almost impeached and that he resigned under that circumstance. His legacy was tarnished for all time.

The heroes in this pivotal event were Woodward and Bernstein, who were assigned to cover that break-in at the Watergate. Journalism realized its highest point in history because of them. Students from all over the country wanted to be investigative reporters after the Watergate reporting.

Ford's time in the White House was short. He served from August 1974 to January 1977. Resentments from both sides remain. Many Republicans might claim that Nixon got a bad deal. Democrats would say that Nixon fought the Constitution over and over again.

Jimmy Carter's time as president was a little less than twice as long as Ford's. Carter had a number of disasters, including interest rates reaching double-digits and not resolving the crisis of Americans being held hostage in Iran for 444 days. Those two problems for Carter cleared the way for former California Governor Ronald Reagan to take over the conservative reins of the Republican Party and the country.

CONCLUSIONS

Richard Nixon wanted to be president of the United States. While considered by most to be an intelligent man, he was hardly popular even in his own party. After losing to Kennedy in 1960, he seemed to blame the world at large and threatened to never run for office again, certainly not for the presidency. But given the damage done in 1964 by Goldwater and the apparent vacuum in party leadership, Nixon ran in 1968 and won.

Except for the problem of the conflict in Vietnam, Nixon did an effective job in his first term. His re-election appeared to be a "slam dunk" in

1972. But he took the anti-war protests personally. In addition, he happened to be engulfed in the biggest culture change in American history, given the civil rights protests and the women's movement. As a result he wanted to ensure that he was re-elected.

When burglars broke into the Watergate Building, few people realized that was the beginning of the end for Nixon. While it was the Democrats who brought about charges that could have resulted in impeachment, the true investigators were the reporters for the *Washington Post*. It was the press that brought Watergate to the politicians' attention. The element of fear was there, and Nixon thought they were all trying to "get him into trouble" despite the fact that it was his actions, especially the attempted cover-up that triggered his demise.

However, the 1972 election became the first overt case of attribution theory in modern American politics. Although largely overlooked by the press at the time, Nixon's justification for the Plumbers unit was to blame Democrats for starting the problem in 1960 through the actions of Dick Tuck. The argument never worked with the public, mainly because few people had any idea who Dick Tuck was or what he had done. Still, a precedent had been set.

REFERENCES

Bernstein, C., & Woodward, B. (1973, June 3). Dean alleges Nixon knew of cover-up plan. *Washington Post*. Retrieved from http://www.washingtonpost.com/wp-srv/politics/special/watergate/timeline.html.

Carter, D. T. (2000). *The politics of rage: George Wallace, the origins of the new conservatism, and the transformation of American politics*. New York: Simon & Schuster.

Kilpatrick, C. (1973, October 21). Nixon orders firing of Cox; Richardson, Ruckelshaus quit: president abolishes prosecutor's office; FBI seals records, *Washington Post*. Retrieved from http://www.washingtonpost.com/wp-srv/politics/special/watergate/timeline.html.

Lardner, G. Jr. (1973, May 19). Cox is chosen special prosecutor. *Washington Post*. Retrieved from http://www.washingtonpost.com/wp-srv/politics/special/watergate/timeline.html.

Lewis, A. E. (1972, June 18). 5 held in plot to bug Democrats' office here. *Washington Post*. Retrieved from http://www.washingtonpost.com/wp-srv/politics/special/watergate/timeline.html.

Meyer, L. (1973a, January 31). Last two guilty in Watergate plot. *Washington Post*. Retrieved from http://www.washingtonpost.com/wp-srv/politics/special/watergate/timeline.html.

Meyer, L. (1973b, July 17). President taped talks, phone calls; lawyer ties Ehrlichman to payments. *Washington Post*. Retrieved from http://www.washingtonpost.com/wp-srv/politics/special/watergate/timeline.html.

Sheehan, N. (1971). *The Pentagon papers*. New York: Quadrangle.

Stern, L., & Johnson, H. (1973, May 1). 3 top Nixon aides, Kleindienst out; president accepts full responsibility; Richardson will conduct new probe. *Washington Post*. Retrieved from http://www.washingtonpost.com/wp-srv/politics/special/watergate/timeline.html.

Woodward, B., & Bernstein, C. (1972a, June 19). GOP security aide among five arrested in bugging affair. *Washington Post.* Retrieved from http://www.washingtonpost.com/wp-srv/politics/special/watergate/timeline.html.

Woodward, B., & Bernstein, C. (1972b, August 1). Bug suspect got campaign funds. *Washington Post.* Retrieved from http://www.washingtonpost.com/wp-srv/politics/special/watergate/timeline.html.

Woodward, B., & Bernstein, C. (1972c, September 29). Mitchell controlled secret GOP fund. *Washington Post.* Retrieved from http://www.washingtonpost.com/wp-srv/politics/special/watergate/timeline.html.

Woodward, B, & Bernstein, C. (1972d, October 10). FBI finds Nixon aides sabotaged Democrats. *Washington Post.* Retrieved from http://www.washingtonpost.com/wp-srv/politics/special/watergate/timeline.html.

Woodward, B., & Bernstein, C. (1973, June 13). Break-in memo sent to Ehrlichman. *Washington Post.* Retrieved from http://www.washingtonpost.com/wp-srv/politics/special/watergate/timeline.html.

SIX

1980: Ronald Reagan and the Southern Strategy (Once Again)

The 1980 campaign opened at a dark time for the nation's economy and foreign policy under the incumbent president, Jimmy Carter. On the home front, people were dealing with double-digit interest rates for their mortgages. Homeowners with flexible mortgages saw their payments double or worse. Those trying to buy new homes were hit with high interest rates which barred them from qualifying for loans. The down-turn in the housing market meant that retailers had trouble selling their inventories. That, in turn, led to a decline in manufacturing output.

On the international scene, a group of Americans were held hostage at their embassy in Iran. One attempted rescue mission failed when one of the helicopters carrying troops was disabled by sand in the Iranian desert. Essentially, the United States looked weak at home and abroad.

Into the breach stepped former actor and California governor Ronald Reagan, an unsuccessful candidate for his party's nomination four years earlier. Reagan entered the campaign with a double advantage. Not only was incumbent Carter unpopular, but Reagan was also gifted with the dramatic and rhetorical skills of an actor—something that Carter lacked on both fronts.

TICKET SPLITTING

One technique that Reagan employed was a variation on a common strategy used by Republicans called Ticket Splitting. The Ticket Splitting strategy was developed by DeVries and Tarrance (1972) as a way to maximize Republican chances in places where Democrats had an edge in party registration. The approach sought to identify those Democrats who had a tendency to vote split tickets, i.e., voting for both some Democrat and some Republican candidates for various offices in the same election. DeVries and Tarrance even identified the demographic group most open to ticket splitting—younger voters who had more education than most voters and who lived in the suburbs. In addition, the ticket splitter consumed more media than most voters and was more politically active than those who voted straight Democratic tickets. Thus this voter was viewed as a fairly complex voter who was knowledgeable about campaign issues. Ultimately, ticket splitters were attracted to candidates whom they viewed as problem solvers instead of being drawn to candidates because of their political affiliation.

Prior to 1980, most Republican campaigns had targeted the ticket splitter. Reagan's campaign, however, employed a major revision of the strategy. His campaign wanted to target Southern Democrats who lived in rural areas, a group of voters who had little in common with the suburban ticket splitters aimed at in most previous campaigns. One campaign, Gil Carmichael's Mississippi race for the U.S Senate in the 1970s, had tried a similar approach. It partially worked, with Carmichael doing well with the state's rural voters but still losing the election (Powell & Flick, 1994).

The basis of Reagan's strategy was somewhat different. Those rural Southern Democrats could be reached, the thinking went, if they were targeted with messages that appealed directly to them. Further, the 1964 Goldwater election showed what message worked with those voters— something with racial overtones. Reagan altered it slightly, using attacks on welfare (and its recipients) as a coded version that would both appeal to rural white voters and encourage them to turn out.

IMPLICIT RACISM AT THE NESHOBA COUNTY FAIR

That message was reinforced when Reagan made his first major presidential campaign speech, following the 1980 Republican Convention, at the Neshoba County Fair near Philadelphia, Mississippi. The town of Philadelphia, the county seat of Neshoba, had a remarkable place in Mississippi history. It was well known for its high school football team, producing such players as 1959 Heisman Trophy winner Billy Cannon (De-Gravelles, 2015) and the highly sought-after recruit Marcus Dupree (Morris, 1992). Its music history included country music performer Marty Stuart. The city was also home to the remaining members of the Choctaw Native American tribe.

But Philadelphia is best known for its infamous history in the civil rights movement. In June 1964, during the height of the movement, three volunteers (two white, one African American) disappeared after being arrested and briefly held in the town's jail. The recovery of their bodies sparked national outrage.

Much of those events probably seemed like ancient history by the time Reagan spoke at the Neshoba County Fair in 1980, but that sense of "things past" was multiplied because few people in the county ever spoke about the killings for decades. In fact, the prosecution of a key member in the group that killed the three men did not occur until 2005; Edgar Ray Killen was sentenced to 20 years in prison for his role in the murders. The first black mayor was not elected in the city until 2009. Thus, in 1980, the city of Philadelphia was still in denial about its racial past.

Ronald Reagan stepped into that situation on August 3, one day after he spoke at the National Urban League meeting in New York (Shirley, 2009). The speech at Neshoba was essentially his first public speech following the Republican National Convention. The location was only a few miles from where James Chaney, Andrew Goodman, and Michael Schwerner had been killed. The setting was entirely too uncomfortable for Reagan consultant and pollster, Dick Wirthlin, who tried to talk the candidate out of making the appearance.

But Reagan insisted. And his topic was states' rights, a term that had been used in the 1960s by George Wallace and others as a euphemism for maintaining segregation. Reagan openly spoke of the concept, without mentioning segregation or anything negative about African Americans. "I believe in states' rights . . . ," he said. "I believe we have distorted the balance of our government today by giving powers that were never intended to be given in the Constitution to that federal establishment." He ended with a vow to "restore to states and local governments the power that properly belongs to them" (Herbert, 2007, A29).

The speech drew national attention for its covert appeal to southern white voters. As Shirley (2009) noted, "The media leveled Reagan for using the phrase 'states' rights' . . . because some saw it as a code phrase for racism" (392). That's likely a good interpretation of how the Mississippi voters in his audience viewed the term. And, while Reagan had his own twist on the topic, critics thought it was eerily similar to Richard Nixon's southern strategy in 1968 and 1972.

Despite its importance in the 1980 campaign, the speech at the Neshoba County Fair has received little attention from Reagan biographers. It's not even mentioned in Shirley's (2005) book about the Reagan revolution, nor is it mentioned in Nancy Reagan's (1989) memoir. Even the Reagan campaign backed off the appearance, leaking word to the press that the appearance at the fair was a mistake because "the symbolism and history were just too burdensome, especially for a conservative trying to fight off false charges of racism" (Shirley, 2009, 392).

THE NEW MESSAGE: ATTACKING WELFARE

With the states' rights message discarded, the Reagan campaign needed another message for targeting southern white Democrats. The campaign found it in conservative attacks on welfare, with the topic providing an implicit message that he was talking about African American voters who lived on welfare checks. At the explicit level, the message was an argument about waste and fraud in federal allocations. The argument was basically straightforward. Fiscal responsibility required that the nation live under a balanced budget. The most obvious place to look for savings was in social programs. Money could be saved, the message argued, if those people who abused the welfare system could be eliminated as recipients (Pierson, 1995). Or, as O'Reilly and Dugard (2015) wrote, Reagan was "eager to break" the nation "out of the cradle-to-grave welfare philosophy" that existed among many of the nation's poor (96).

With voters who had opposed FDR's "welfare state" approach to government, Reagan's words rang true. By 1980, the number of voters who had benefitted from the New Deal were few and far between. In the minds of these new voters, Roosevelt had initiated a never-ending bequest to the poor. Unlike FDR's government work programs, these recipients didn't even have to work. The perception, too, was that the vast majority of recipients were black. They weren't in reality, but the perception remained.

Reagan's most popular version of the message was a fictitious story about a supposed "welfare queen" who stole $150,000 from the federal government. The story, as Reagan told it, was about a woman who drove a Cadillac and was sometimes seen with her poodle at the grocery store buying cigarettes and beer or wine with food stamps. She has been seen in every state. In some places that were not concerned with political correctness at the time, they mentioned that she was an African American.

This story was first presented to the American public in a 1976 campaign speech by Reagan, and he repeated it in his 1980 campaign. The woman allegedly accumulated her wealth by using 80 aliases, 30 addresses, a dozen Social Security cards, and four fictional dead husbands ("'Welfare queen' becomes issue . . .," 1976). That anecdote was likely triggered by an earlier top ten country song called "Welfare Cadillac," written by Guy Drake (1970). The story is a typical "dependency narrative" aimed at attacking those viewed as taking money from the government (Cassiman, 2006). This legend has been thoroughly debunked (Seccombe, 2010), with at least one scholar saying the story was created as a way to stigmatize welfare (Kohler-Hausman, 2007). Reagan's response was that the nation's racial problems had been solved in the 1960s and claims of racial problems at the time were merely a result of complaints by African-American leaders and teachers (Pettigrew, 1999).

Regardless of its fictional nature, it worked. Reagan easily defeated Carter, thanks partly to his ability to attract white voters in southern states. In addition, the white rural voters in those southern states became consistent Republican voters for decades to follow. The only state that Carter won was his native Georgia.

HELP FROM THE EVANGELICALS

Reagan also benefitted from the first true organized efforts to encourage conservative religious groups to mobilize on behalf of Republican candidates. Religion and American politics had always been intertwined at some level, but that association was mostly an informal arrangement prior to the 1980 campaign. Into that breach stepped a conservative Baptist preacher from Virginia named Jerry Falwell. Falwell used his syndicated television show, the "Old Time Gospel Hour," to form a new religious-political group called the Moral Majority. As Winters (2012) noted, "Falwell did not eliminate the line between religion and politics. Nor did he blur it. He jumped over it, bringing millions of voters with him" (12). In effect, Falwell almost single-handedly crystallized the evangelical movement behind Republican candidates. As Winters added, evangelicals "became not only a part of the Reagan Revolution but an integral constituency of the Republican Party" (6). For the 1980 election, the math was simple. Reagan took 61 percent of the white evangelical vote in the nation. This, despite the fact that Carter was well known as a Sunday school teacher in rural Georgia.

It is important to note that although LBJ's civil rights proposals integrated many institutions across the country, most churches were not among them. Although race was not part of the church argument, the implications were there as well.

Subsequent studies have indicated that the financial backing for the Moral Majority and other groups did not always come from the kind of small donations that Falwell solicited on his television show. Much of it came, it turns out, from a handful of billionaires who saw a chance to use such conservative groups to back their personal causes (Mayer, 2016). In fact, much of Falwell's money was raised by Paul Weyrich, who co-founded the Moral Majority with the preacher. Weyrich operated a direct-mail firm that raised money for the organization. But Weyrich's firm was heavily supported by Richard Mellon Scaife, an heir to the Mellon fortune, which came from ancestors who had founded Mellon banking, Alcoa Aluminum, and Gulf Oil.

To evangelical voters, though, none of that mattered. What mattered was that God was a Republican, and it was the duty of believers to turn out and vote for Republican candidates. Post-election analysis indicated that the evangelical vote added at least five to six percentage points to

Reagan's margin of victory (Brudney & Copeland, 1984). It was a trend that would continue through the 1980s, the 1990s, and beyond (Clyde, DeBell & Sigelman, 1999).

MORE HELP FROM PACS

One final factor entered into the 1980 election that was a major boost to the Reagan campaign: the role of political action committees (PACs) (Busch, 2005). The role of Super PACs in modern elections will be discussed in more detail in a later chapter. What's important to remember in relation to the 1980 election is that the impact of such PACs is not new. The most active and successful PAC in 1980 was the National Conservative Political Action Committee, or NCPAC (pronounced Nick-pack). NCPAC became the first major political action committee to actively participate and communicate with voters in a direct manner (Kitchens & Powell, 1986). They were primarily active in statewide campaigns, but their efforts led to an increased turnout of Republican voters in the states where they were engaged. They used a simple formula of communicating primarily with direct mail and television ads, often using the same ads only with the difference of changing the names of the candidates (Smith, et al., 2010). Further, while there were other conservative groups that were also active in the campaign (e.g., the American Security Council, the Moral Majority, and the Eagle Forum), NCPAC served as a central organization to orchestrate opposition to Democratic candidates. And, perhaps even more importantly, the entire movement represented a redefinition of American conservatism (Wilbanks, 1983).

Although Richard Viguerie (1980) founded NCPAC in 1975, the 1980 election became its first major test. The major focus of its campaign was its "Target '80" program aimed at defeating six incumbent Democratic senators—Birch Bayh (Indiana), Alan Cranston (California), Thomas Eagleton (Missouri), Frank Church (Idaho), John Culver (Iowa), and George McGovern (South Dakota). Four of those candidates—Bayh, Church, Culver, and McGovern—were defeated. Subsequent research indicated that the ads produced by the group were indeed effective at defeating those incumbents (Boydston & Kaid, 1983).

A basic tenet of its approach was the articulation of specific messages. Viguerie himself, in talking about conservative voters, wrote:

> They're not really interested in politics. . . . They are interested in the Panama Canal not being given away, reduction of their taxes, a strong national defense, cutting waste and abuse in government programs. That's how people get involved in politics (quoted by Ridgeway, 1982, 15–16).

Perhaps even more important was the valence with which these messages were articulated. There was no room for middle ground. Every message took on equal importance as the mantra of the extreme right wing of the party. That approach was based on research that found that extremity of position was an asset with conservative audiences, and that approach was particularly effective when making negative arguments against incumbents. As Terry Dolan, one architect of the group's strategy wrote:

> I'm convinced that you can say almost anything . . . you could, in fact, *lie*. I think the attention span of the voting population, and the fact that there is no connection between us and any candidate makes that perfectly possible and makes this whole thing open to incredible abuse (quoted in "NCPAC's negative campaign," 1979, 3, italics added).

"A group like ours could lie through their teeth and the candidate it helps stays clean," Dolan said on another occasion (quoted by McPherson, 1980, F1). And, perhaps to no one's surprise, NCPAC did exactly that. One ad against Bayh accused him of voting for a cut in the defense budget, when the senator had actually been absent for that vote (Bannon, 1982). An ad against Church showed an empty silo and said the silo had no missile because of Church's vote; that silo was actually empty because it had contained an obsolete missile. Church also got criticized for a nonexistent vote that the group claimed he made in support of a pay raise for himself (Weinraub, 1980).

As noted earlier, one difference in the third-party attacks by NCPAC and the current role of Super PACs is that NCPAC played no major role in the presidential campaign. Instead, the only direct advantage that the Reagan campaign got from NCPAC was increased voter turnout by Republicans in the states in which they were active. Still, NCPAC demonstrated the potential advantage of third-party attacks in a campaign. It was the foundation for the Swift Boat Veterans campaign against John Kerry in 2004 and for Karl Rove's Super PACs in subsequent campaigns.

CONCLUSIONS

In retrospect, Reagan's election in 1980 was likely due to the poor economic conditions that existed in the nation during the Carter administration (Hibbs Jr., 1982); thus the pillar of consumerism was a major factor. In addition, the 1980 campaign marked one of the first overt appeals to religious conservatives in presidential elections, a factor that made religion an important pillar. However, the perceptions of the campaign may have been more important. For Republicans, the election was the beginning of the Reagan revolution, a movement that continues to inspire modern Republicans. Further, that campaign also set the stage for the partisan polarization that still shackles American democracy today. Reagan used implicit racial messages to appeal to southern segregationists while blaming Democrats for the nation's woes. He also got help from evangelical voters in a voting trend that continues to benefit Republicans. And finally, Reagan benefitted from the ethically questionable, independent campaigns of political action committees, a trend that has expanded dramatically with the *Citizens United* ruling by the Supreme Court, which dealt with the regulation of campaign spending by organizations. As a result, Ronald Reagan's 1980 campaign became a prototypical approach used by future Republican candidates as they sought to expand the hold that the party had on the nation.

REFERENCES

Bannon, B. (1982). NCPAC's role in the 1980 Senate elections. *Campaign & Elections, 3,* 43–46.

Boydston, J., & Kaid, L. L. (1983). *An experimental study of the effectiveness of NCPAC's political advertisements.* Paper presented at the annual meeting of the Southern Speech Communication Association, Orlando.

Brudney, J. L., & Copeland, G. W. (1984). Evangelicals as a political force: Reagan and the 1980 religious vote. *Social Science Quarterly, 65(4),* 1072–1079.

Busch, A. E. (2005). *Reagan's victory: The presidential election of 1980 and the rise of the right.* Lawrence: University Press of Kansas.

Cassiman, S. A. (2008). Resisting the neo-liberal poverty discourse: On constructing deadbeat dads and welfare queens. Sociology Compass, 2(5), 1690–1700.

Clyde, W., DeBell, M., & Sigelman, L. (1999). The second coming of the new Christian right: Patterns of popular support in 1984 and 1996. *Social Science Quarterly, 80(1),* 181–192.

DeGravelles, C. N. (2015). *Billy Cannon: A long, long run.* Baton Rouge: Louisiana State University Press.

DeVries, W., & Tarrance, L. (1972). *The ticket-splitter: A new force in American politics.* Grand Rapids, MI: Eerdmans.

Drake, G. (1970). Welfare Cadillac. *Royal American Music.*

Herbert, B. (2007). Righting Reagan's wrongs. *New York Times,* A29.

Hibbs Jr., D. A. (1982). President Reagan's mandate from 1980 elections. *American Politics Quarterly, 10(4),* 387–420.

Kitchens, J. T., & Powell, L. (1986). A critical analysis of NCPAC's strategies in key 1980 races: A third-party negative campaign. *Southern Speech Communication Journal, 51,* 208–228.

Kohler-Hausman, J. (2007). The crime of survival: Fraud prosecutions, community surveillance, and the original 'Welfare Queen.' *Journal of Social History, 41,* 329–354.

Mayer, J. (2016). *Dark money: The hidden history of the billionaires behind the rise of the radical right.* New York: Doubleday.

McPherson, M. (1980, August 10). The New Right brigade. *Washington Post,* F1.

Morris, W. (1992). *The courting of Marcus Dupree,* Jackson: University Press of Mississippi.

NCPAC's negative campaign (1979). *Political Action Report, 5,* 1–3.

O'Reilly, B., & Dugard, M. (2015). *Killing Reagan: The violent assault that changed a presidency.* New York: Henry Holt.

Pettigrew, T. F. (1999). Sociological analyses confront fashionable racial fallacies. *Sociological Forum, 14,* 177–184.

Pierson, P. (1995). *Dismantling the welfare state? Reagan, Thatcher and the politics of retrenchment.* Cambridge, MA: Cambridge University Press.

Powell, L., & Flick, H. (1994). *Ticket splitting in Mississippi.* Paper presented at the annual meeting of the Southern Speech Communication Association, Hot Springs, AK.

Reagan, N. (1989). *My turn: The memoirs of Nancy Reagan.* New York: Random House.

Ridgeway, J. (1982, June 20). The men who stuff your mailbox. *Parade,* 15–16.

Seccombe, K. (2010). *So you think I drive a Cadillac? Welfare recipients perspectives on the system and its reforms* (3rd ed.). Boston: Pearson.

Shirley, C. (2005). *Reagan's revolution: The untold story of the campaign that started it all.* Nashville: Thomas Nelson.

Shirley, C. (2009). *Rendezvous with destiny: Ronald Reagan and the campaign that changed America.* Wilmington, DE: ISI Books.

Smith, M., Williams, G. C., Powell, L., & Copeland, G. (2010). *Campaign finance reform: The political shell game.* Lanham, MD: Lexington.

Viguerie, R. (1980). *The New Right: We're ready to lead.* Falls Church, VA: Viguerie Company.

Weinraub, B. (1980, May 11). Oust Church drive in Idaho stirs smear tactics. *New York Times,* A20.

'Welfare queen' becomes issue in Reagan campaign (1976, February 15). *New York Times,* A51.

Wilbanks, C. (1983). *Ronald Reagan and the New Right: A study in spacious rhetoric.* Paper presented at the annual meeting of the Southern Speech Communication Association, Orlando.

Winters, M. S. (2012). *God's right hand: How Jerry Falwell made God a Republican and baptized the American right.* New York: HarperOne.

SEVEN

1992: Bill Clinton and Republican Hatred

The keynote speaker for the Democratic Convention in 1988 was William Jefferson Clinton, the former governor of Arkansas. His speech, expected to be about 15 minutes long, was actually 33 minutes long. At the time, few remembered much about the speech other than it was long. Clinton supported Michael Dukakis in the Democrats' campaign against George H. W. Bush, Reagan's vice president. The length of Clinton's speech and other characteristics of the speech seemed to end any hope of his ever getting into national politics. But his time was only four years away.

Dukakis lost the 1988 election to Bush by a landslide. Though not as bad as the Goldwater and McGovern disasters, Dukakis lost by more than 300 electoral votes, seven million popular votes, and 30 states. The other candidates for the nomination included several individuals who would continue to have an impact on American politics, some in a much more successful way. They included two future vice presidents, Al Gore (Tennessee) and Joe Biden (Delaware). Gary Hart (Colorado), who had been a close aide to McGovern, disappeared from the winner's list when he challenged the press to prove that he was having an affair and the press accommodated. In the primaries Dukakis received the most delegates, followed by Jesse Jackson, the black civil rights minister who had become the voice of the cause following the death of Martin Luther King, Jr. Most of Jackson's delegates had come from southern states where the vast majority of Democratic votes came from African Americans. Though African Americans held the majority of Democratic votes in the southern states, whites outnumbered them in the general election.

Republicans were strongly in favor of Bush. In large measure, Bush's support came from the fact that he had been Reagan's vice president for eight years. Reagan was one of the most popular presidents in the 20th century and probably the most popular among Republicans for decades, and perhaps the entire 20th century.

During Bush's first term, a number of significant events took place. Primary among them was the dissolution of the Soviet Union and the consequent commencement of the post–Cold War period. In 1989, the Soviets had ended their war in Afghanistan, which could have been a forecast of things to come. Even with the Soviets' military strength, they were still unable to defeat local warriors who were familiar with the geography. This Soviet action did not prevent the United States from entering into a fray in Afghanistan in 2002, just 13 years later. Bush banned the importation of certain guns into the United States, which he deemed "assault weapons." Oliver North, a military man who had worked in the Reagan–Bush administration, was convicted of what was referred to as the Iran–Contra affair, involving weapons and drugs, but he was later given immunity for providing additional information to authorities. In the largest protest in Chinese history since Mao, protesters were killed in Tiananmen Square. In December, the United States invaded Panama to depose Manuel Noriega. He was captured and taken to Florida, where he was tried, convicted, and imprisoned.

In 1990, Poland declared the abolishment of a socialist system and withdrew from the Warsaw Pact. Lithuania also protested the Soviet bloc. Nelson Mandela was released from prison in South Africa. An agreement was reached for the reunification of Germany. The Soviet Union withdrew from Czechoslovakia. The Soviet Union, now minus Poland, East Germany, and Czechoslovakia, voted to have an American-style presidency, and elected Mikhail Gorbachev as its leader. Estonia returned to its earlier name, implying its separation from the Soviet Union. The US and the USSR agreed to cease developing chemical weapons. Romania separated from the USSR and held elections. For many, these actions were viewed as the peaceful downfall of the Soviet Union.

In August 1990, the United Nations initiated a trade embargo against Iraq four days after the Iraqis invaded Kuwait. A day later, Bush ordered planes and ships into the Mideast region anticipating an invasion of Iraq. Another day later, Iraq announced its annexation of Kuwait. A month later, in October, Bush announced that the United States would remove Iraqi troops from Kuwait.

In 1992, Clinton offered himself as a candidate for president. At the Democratic Convention in New York City, Clinton won the nomination. Jerry Brown, former governor of California, came in second, but the vote tally was not even close. Clinton chose Senator Al Gore of Tennessee as his running mate. The two campaigned against George H. W. Bush and Dan Quayle, who were running for their second term. The Republicans had held the presidency for 12 consecutive years and were shooting for 16. In one of the few elections where a third-party candidate had much of an impact on the election, Ross Perot, an entrepreneur from Texas, ran for the presidency (Klein, 2003).

Bush signed the Americans with Disabilities Act (ADA). The provisions indicated that certain structural aspects of buildings and public transportation should accommodate people with disabilities.

Bush could claim several positive changes that had taken place in foreign policy. The Soviet Union was breaking up. Germany was reunified. A chemical weapons deal was completed between Gorbachev and Bush. The Iraqi invasion of Kuwait had been quelled, and Saddam Hussein's authority in the Middle East had been decimated by America's quick victory. The Iraqi military that had been lauded by many turned out to be a group of amateurs who retreated in light of the American bombings. An agreement was made to have an outside group monitor Iraq's building of weapons and a no-fly zone was created.

PRESENCE OF THE THIRD PARTY

Ross Perot was an electronics entrepreneur from Texas. His companies had a variety of names including Texas Instruments, which made handheld calculators, as part of Electronic Data Systems (EDS). Perot announced his campaign for the presidency live on the *Larry King Show* on the Cable News Network (CNN). Although Perot had disagreed with Reagan and Bush about a number of issues, it was his focus on the economy that allowed Clinton a pathway to the White House. Perot was in favor of raising gasoline taxes and decreasing Social Security benefits. He was concerned about the growing deficit and the national debt. For example, the national debt had decreased from the end of World War II until 1980. During the Reagan administration, the debt had increased despite mostly peacetime economies. Reagan's and Bush's answer to some of the lingering problems brought about during the Carter administration had been to lower the interest rate but in the process had raised the national debt. Most agreed that Perot had little chance of winning the election, but many thought that Perot's entering the election would take away votes from Bush.

Clinton was a lightning rod for criticism from the beginning of the campaign, drawing either very positive or very negative responses. The negatives included the nickname "Slick Willie." Republicans focused on his alleged penchant for sexual relations outside of his marriage. The first assertion was that Clinton had an affair with Gennifer Flowers in the 1970s. Flowers and two others, Paula Jones and Monica Lewinsky, eventually surfaced as women whom Clinton had relations with before and during his presidency. Clinton was criticized for not serving in the military during the Vietnam War. While Bush had fought during World War II, Clinton had studied as a Fulbright Scholar at Oxford during the Vietnam War. He noted that he had smoked marijuana but "never actually inhaled." The Flowers story and the military service story caused his popularity to decrease substantially in early 1992. Other candidates were winning primaries in different states, usually in states that were near their home or in their home state. The marijuana issue apparently had little impact, especially because so many Americans, including veterans of Vietnam, had smoked the substance. The other allegations remained, but Clinton won the Georgia primary in March (Klein, 1996).

That victory was an indication of Clinton's favorability among black voters. It is somewhat interesting that Clinton and Jimmy Carter found acceptance in the South, despite the fact that they were Democrats. Clinton's obvious southern accent and the fact that people knew he was from Arkansas gave him credibility in the South despite those voters not agreeing with his views.

Clinton took somewhat of a "pop culture" approach in the campaign appearing on the *Arsenio Hall Show* on late night television, where he played the saxophone. Even at convention time, Clinton was losing the election in national polls to Ross Perot.

THE CONVENTIONS AND BEYOND

Clinton won the Democratic nomination. There was little controversy, except that the Democrats did not allow anti-abortion advocates to speak at the convention. With that, Democrats began their decades' long pro-choice stance. Al Gore of Tennessee was selected as the nominee for vice president. Clinton escaped the allegations concerning Gennifer Flowers for the time being. Clinton and his wife, Hillary, appeared on CBS's *60 Minutes*. They neither admitted nor denied the allegations. Their waffling answers to questions hinged on their claim to privacy in family issues, a claim which they insisted most other Americans would make as well. Clinton actually won the election with a majority of women voters, despite his reputation (Miller & Shanks, 1996).

There were no problems for George H. W. Bush at the convention. However, the poor economy was his issue for the upcoming general election.

In July 1992, Ross Perot temporarily dropped out of the election amid some issues regarding his own privacy, but he later re-entered.

While in his first term, Bush had violated his campaign promise of 1988 in which he stated vehemently "No new taxes!" Bush had an early lead, but the economy was getting worse and worse. Issues of the economy were brought up by both Clinton and Perot. In many ways, the debates were two against one, but it wasn't Perot and Bush against Clinton. It was Clinton and Perot against Bush. Perot especially was concerned about passing the proposed NAFTA (the North American Free Trade

Agreement) claiming that it would create a "giant sucking sound." The three debates were all held in October, about a month before the election. The proximity of the debates to the election probably infused a greater impact than in other years.

Bush made two significant gaffes during the debates. On one occasion, he looked at his watch. That behavior to some was an indication that he did not care about the debate. The second, and most significant, was when he attempted to answer a question from a black woman who wanted to know how the recession economy affected him *personally*. Bush waffled with the question and was never able to state any particular way that he had been affected. By glazing over the question, for the woman who asked it and for many others, it meant that Bush had no empathy for the people who were truly hurt by the economy. When Clinton responded in empathic terms, he never really answered it either. However, the general opinion was that Clinton cared and Bush did not (Smith, 1994).

In the election Clinton drew more than twice the electoral votes as Bush. Clinton won a few southern states, but Bush maintained the Solid South for the most part. Clinton's southern drawl and the fact that he was from Arkansas and his running mate, Al Gore, was from Tennessee helped him secure more than enough votes. Clinton, however, focused on particular states using strategies developed by campaign strategist James Carville and others. It was noticeable that Clinton was drawing more in urban areas and areas with large educated populaces, such as college towns. This would become a landmark for what we now refer to as red states (predominantly Republican and conservative) and blue states (predominantly Democratic and liberal). In large measure, one could even talk about red counties and blue counties. The 1992 election also provided some insights for the future. Places with significant Hispanic populations voted for Democrats, including Bush's native state, Texas.

For Clinton, though, winning the primaries and the election may have been his easiest tasks. In June of his first year, Clinton ordered an attack on Iraq because the Iraqis had planned an attack on former president Bush while he was visiting Kuwait. In December, Clinton signed the North American Free Trade Agreement (NAFTA), the program that Perot had vehemently opposed as a candidate. Progress was being made in several different ways, but the Republican plan to "Get Clinton" had begun early in his presidency.

THE "GET CLINTON" CAMPAIGN

As we have stated, Clinton had already been labelled "Slick Willie," and opponents were geared up to ensure that he would at least have only one term—and perhaps less. Clinton created additional opposition early in his presidency. Within his first month in office, Clinton eliminated restrictions on abortions that had been imposed by Reagan and Bush. In addition, he selected his wife, Hillary Rodham Clinton, to serve in a position to undertake health care reforms. The Republicans created massive campaigns to get Clinton out of office as soon as they could. They were threatened and feared that other historic Democratic ideas would come into play and somewhat concerned that Clinton would be the one who could implement them.

Travelgate

Like almost every issue since Watergate, controversies have ended in "gate." Travelgate was Clinton's first issue after taking office. Clinton fired seven members of the White House Travel staff. Although Clinton had a right to do so, it had been precedent that the White House maintained the staff from one presidency to another. They were allegedly fired because of "improprieties" undertaken by the staff in previous presidencies. The accusation against Clinton about this act was that he fired the staffers because he wanted to give the travel business to friends of his from Arkansas. Among the issues looked into by independent counsel Kenneth Starr, this one found nothing illegal on the part of the Clintons. Yet the issue remained in the public venue from 1993 to 1998.

Whitewater and Vince Foster's Death

Whitewater was a land development project in Arkansas. The Clintons invested in the property. The FBI looked into a scandal regarding an Arkansas bank and loans involving the property and the law firm where Hillary Rodham Clinton had practiced. Although the Clintons were never formally charged with anything, the Republicans pushed forward with the scandal. In August 1994, Starr was appointed by a three-judge panel to look into the matter. When asked to provide documents related to Whitewater, the Clintons were unable to find them. Many, however, thought the documents had been in the office of Clinton friend and White House counsel, Vince Foster. Foster was from Bill Clinton's hometown of Hope.

Vince Foster was found dead and an autopsy revealed that he had committed suicide by shooting himself in the mouth. Republicans were not convinced that his death was a suicide and took part in promoting conspiracies that Bill Clinton himself had been involved in a conspiracy to murder Foster. In 1997, Starr concluded that Foster's death was suicide, after several years of investigation. Even so, the conspiracy campaign was significant. The conservatives found that they could keep an issue in the public eye for years, especially with the assistance of conservative radio talk show hosts. In this case, there was little concern about the final outcome of an investigation. The concern was to maintain a negative feeling in the public that the President was doing something wrong, at least unethical, if not illegal. Attempts at claiming that there were files in Vince Foster's office that had been removed after his death, regarding the Whitewater event subsided, but only years after the investigations started. This episode was referred to as "Filegate." The use of "___-gate" was an attempt to codify charges against the Clintons as actions similar to those of Nixon in the Watergate scandal.

Paula Jones

Paula Jones was another of Clinton's "Arkansas connections." In 1994, two days before the statute of limitations would run out, Jones filed a civil lawsuit against Clinton. She stated that in 1991 Clinton invited her to a hotel room where he exposed himself and propositioned her. The judge ruled for a summary judgment for Clinton because there were no damages. Jones appealed the case, and in that process called for a deposition from Clinton. Clinton's lawyers argued that a sitting president should not be forced to provide a deposition while in office. The conservative Supreme Court unanimously ruled against Clinton. Jones' attorney, Gilbert Davis, was apparently handling the case to gain publicity for a later campaign for attorney general of Virginia as well as for the fees he would receive. Clinton did give the deposition, which by then created a precedent for chief executives to be legally forced to participate in a civil lawsuit where they were defendants. Once again the case was dismissed. Once again she appealed. In 1998, seven years after the allegations began, Clinton's attorneys settled for $850,000, but without Clinton apologizing. Jones herself received only $200,000; the remainder went to attorneys. A year later, a judge ruled that Clinton had been in contempt of court and that Jones' attorneys would only receive about one-fourth of what they had asked (De Yampert Jr., 2000).

Attorney Davis received less money than he wanted but continued to use the case for his political ambitions. Jones divorced and appeared nude in *Penthouse* magazine. There were no winners in the case, but Clinton was definitely the loser.

Monica Lewinsky

The Paula Jones' lawyers tried to show a pattern of behavior in their case, referring to other women who had made allegations about Clinton. Because the Jones' litigation had gone on for so long, the Lewinsky situation that developed in late 1995 became part of the deposition in the Jones case. Jones' lawyers sought out every potential woman who had claimed to have been sexually involved with Clinton.

Lewinsky was an intern in the White House. In December 1997, Lewinsky was subpoenaed by Jones' lawyers to provide a deposition. Clinton told Lewinsky to be evasive in her responses to questions. In the meantime, Kenneth Starr contacted Attorney General Janet Reno about expanding his role as special prosecutor to include allegations charging Clinton with other crimes. Jones' attorneys provided information about previous trials to Starr, including the deposition of Bill Clinton. Numerous others, including Kathleen Willey, a former White House worker, and Linda Tripp, a colleague of Lewinsky's at the Pentagon, got involved in the trial as well. Starr, at this point, was less focused on the Jones allegations than he was about what happened with Lewinsky. As the Lewinsky situation heated up, it became the joke of the country (Powell & Kitchens, 1999).

It was clear from his actions that Starr had a vendetta against Clinton. Clinton's lawyers continually tried to escape the situation by claiming executive privilege. Kathleen Willey's story was discounted, to some extent, because she tried to profit from a book contract about the issue. Obviously, the entire story was gold for both traditional media and social media. Conservative radio commentators pushed for Clinton to resign or be impeached.

Starr even interviewed Secret Service agents in the Clinton White House despite objections from a number of sources, including former president Bush. Clinton finally agreed to testify to the Grand Jury. Based on information provided by Starr, the House decided there was enough evidence to impeach Clinton. He was convicted of perjury to a Grand Jury and obstruction of justice. The Senate trial began with Chief Justice William Rehnquist presiding. A two-thirds vote was needed to dismiss Clinton from office. On the two charges, most senators voted the same way. Five Republicans voted "not guilty" on both charges. Five voted "guilty" on only one charge. Otherwise the voting was a straight party issue.

THE CLINTON ERA CONTINUES

The Republicans had waited until after the mid-term elections to bring the impeachment issue forward. Speaker of the House Newt Gingrich (R-GA) expected that the Republicans would pick up enough votes to have Clinton removed from office. It did not happen. Gingrich himself resigned. Whether he resigned because he felt guilty about the Clinton impeachment, felt that he had failed his party because of the mid-term elections, or he simply did not want to work with Clinton as president for two more years, or some combination of reasons, Gingrich was gone for Clinton's last two years in office (Harris, 2006).

The continuous charges thrown against Bill Clinton were probably more than any other president had ever encountered. Through it all, his popularity and approval ratings remained about the same (Sonner & Wilcox, 1999). He may have been the most popular president of all time, possibly because of what he endured and how he handled it. Even many of those who might refer to him as "Slick Willie" still admitted he was a gregarious person and effective rhetor. For the 2000 election, Al Gore, Clinton's vice president in both terms, would be the nominee for president. Gore ran against George W. Bush, George H. W. Bush's son. Hillary Clinton, the first lady, also ran for the Senate from New York and won. She became the first first lady elected to office (Powell, Hickson, McCroskey, & Amsbary, 2015).

Still, perhaps the most important attribute of the Clinton administration is that politics had erupted into a clear partisan fight. Clinton was hated by Republicans, and Clinton's supporters hated the GOP. The antagonism reached a climax with impeachment proceedings against the president for his relationship in office with Monica Lewinsky. Technically, the charge was that of perjury, for lying during the subsequent investigation, but the public assumed that it was about the affair itself. Republicans succeeded in painting Clinton in a negative light until information came to light that some members of the impeachment committee, including those who were heavily vocal in attacking Clinton, were themselves individuals who were engaging in illicit love affairs. That led to a dismissal of charges against the president and a general disgust with politicians by the public as a whole. The fingerpointing of blame was under way.

REFERENCES

Harris, J. F. (2006). *The survivor: Bill Clinton in the White House.* New York: Random House.

Klein, J. (2003). *The natural: The misunderstood presidency of Bill Clinton.* New York: Random House Digital.

Klein, J. G. (1996). Negativity in impressions of presidential candidates revisited: The 1992 election. *Personality and Social Psychology Bulletin, 22*(3), 288–295.

Miller, W. E., & Shanks, J. M. (1996). *The new American voter.* Cambridge, MA: Harvard University Press.

Powell, L., & Kitchens, J. T. (1999). Sex and income as factors associated with exposure to jokes about the Clinton-Lewinsky controversy. *Psychological Reports, 84*(3), 1047–1050.

Powell, L., Hickson, M., McCroskey, J. C., & Amsbary, J. (2015). Perceptions of authenticity in the Watergate Hearings. *Journal of Political Science & Public Affairs, 3*(169), 2332–0761.

Smith, S. A. (1994). *Bill Clinton on stump, state, and stage: The rhetorical road to the White House.* Fayetteville: University of Arkansas Press.

Sonner, M. W., & Wilcox, C. (1999). Forgiving and forgetting: Public support for Bill Clinton during the Lewinsky scandal. *PS: Political Science & Politics, 32*(03), 554–557.

De Yampert Jr, J. (2000). Death of constitutional law: A Critique of the *Clinton v. Jones* decision. *Marshall Law Review, 26*, 185.

EIGHT

2000: Bush, Gore, and Florida

Al Gore was in a good position to win a third straight presidential term for the Democrats. The Democrats had come off two consecutive terms with Bill Clinton as president. Admittedly, Clinton faced problems during his terms, with the Monica Lewinsky controversy being the most visible of those issues. Clinton's affair with the office intern had sparked impeachment proceedings (Arthos, 2002; Silva, Jenkins-Smith & Waterman, 2007) and had become the subject of jokes (Kitchens & Powell, 1999). But the impeachment proceedings fell apart.

Meanwhile, the nation's economy had been revived during Clinton's time in office. The federal budget had been balanced, deficit spending was a thing of the past, and the overall economic climate was positive. That was the type of economic environment that was conducive to the same party maintaining control of the presidency for another four years. Further, Al Gore was uniquely situated to take advantage of that situation. After all, he had been the vice president during those heady times.

Meanwhile, the Republican nomination came down to two major candidates, Texas governor George W. Bush (the son of the previous president) and Arizona senator John McCain. McCain held on until he was defeated by a smear campaign in the South Carolina primary. Bush used the momentum from that win to sew up the nomination. However, much of that momentum disappeared due to a number of key missteps by the future president.

The key pillar for the campaign was consumerism. Gore became the advocate for maintaining a healthy economy. Republican Bush basically made the same argument, with the caveat that he could perform that function better than a Democrat.

On election day, Gore won the popular vote. But voting irregularities in South Florida resulted in the outcome of the election going to the

Supreme Court for the first time in history. There, a Republican-dominated court awarded the win to George W. Bush by a 5-to-4 vote. The election was decided, but the animosity between the two parties was growing stronger.

SMEAR CAMPAIGNING

The most notorious smear campaign in this election did not come in the general election, but in a Republican primary—specifically in the South Carolina primary (Bumiller, 2008). The most effective of the rumors appears to have been that Bush's major opponent, John McCain, had fathered a black child and that his wife, Cindy, was a drug addict. As Smith (2016) wrote, "In South Carolina, the race turned ugly" (106). Bush, in trouble after losing the New Hampshire primary to McCain, used "thinly veiled appeals to homophobia, racism, and fundamentalist exclusivity" to win the state (106). Smith went on to say that "The 2000 South Carolina Republican primary was one of the nastiest electoral campaigns on record" (106). And, he added, the voters "were bombarded by robo-calls, telephone banks, emails and anonymous mailings castigating McCain's character" (107).

Not surprisingly, one impact of the election was increased polarization by black and white voters as both parties targeted those voters independently. Gore's campaign focused heavily on trying to achieve a high turnout in African-American voters, particularly in the Jacksonville and South Florida areas. Bush, meanwhile, went after white blue-collar voters and was successful in getting their support. Sheppard (2013), in fact, argued that the 2000 election was the beginning of a major shift in the alignment of this group, with "traditionally Democratic pre-materialist white blue-collar constituencies having moved toward the Republican Party, while the opposite has occurred in traditionally Republican post-materialist suburban constituencies" (272). Sheppard's analysis ran through the 2012 election, but it seems to have continued through the 2016 campaign. Donald Trump was successful at winning the Republican nomination because he had strong support from blue-collar white voters, although he alienated some other white voters who traditionally voted Republican. As analyst Nate Cohn (2016) noted, the 2016 election "has the potential to reshape the allegiances of many white working-class voters who have traditionally sided with the Democrats, and many well-educated voters who have sided with the Republicans" (3).

Why this demographic shift? The cynic would say it was because of covert appeals to racism. The Bush campaign's primary attack against McCain was a racist rumor that he had fathered a black child. Other appeals continued the Reagan argument against welfare, with the implied idea that black voters were more likely to receive welfare payments.

Berman (2015) argued that Bush's basic racist argument in 2000 was an appeal to a "voting-rights counterrevolution" (16).

Regardless, it was the beginning of an increasingly frequent attempt by Republicans to indirectly appeal to white voters. One critic of the 2016 election argued that this racism was central to the success of Trump, noting that "When you do racist [expletive] for decades, over and over, then eventually you get to say it's a racist party. Riling up the base and making this base angry and making it racially charged by dog-whistling endlessly, year after year, has consequences, and this is one of them" (quoted by Piepenburg, 2016, C6). Similarly, *New York Times* columnist Charles M. Blow (2016) wrote, "Trump has used a toxic mix of bullying and bluster, xenophobia and nationalism, misogyny and racism, to appeal to the darker nature of the Republican Party" (A19).

STUMBLES AND MISTAKES ON THE WAY TO VICTORY

George W. Bush was eventually named the winner of the general election. That win was particularly surprising, given the number of mistakes that the Bush campaign made. The mistakes first appeared at the Republican National Convention, where Bush gave one of the worst acceptance speeches in the history of presidential politics. He seemed to be unclear regarding what he wanted to say, stumbled over words and phrases, and generally appeared to be over his head at giving a major political speech. The performance created some anxiety on the part of Republicans, but the problem was relatively simple. Bush was trying to read the speech from a teleprompter without practicing in advance. His problem was that he was reading parts of the sentences that covered one line on the teleprompter, instead of scanning the speaking aid and speaking in complete sentences. Understandably, the audience did not respond well. As Smith (2016) wrote, "The applause was tepid" (163).

Mistakes continued to pile up as the campaign progressed. Most were minor errors, but a few seemed to reflect a man who knew little about domestic or international issues. The most glaring of these was when he called for the privatization of Social Security (Smith, 2016), an idea that did not go well with voters. As Bush tried to defend the concept, he eventually gave a speech in which he indicated that he did not realize Social Security was a federal program. The miscue occurred in a speech in which he argued for allowing Social Security to be taken over and invested by Wall Street firms, but the idea merely triggered fears among older voters who relied on Social Security checks as their only source of income. Smith described the failure of Bush's Social Security plan as a "debacle" for his administration (104).

GEORGE W. BUSH AND THE EVANGELICALS

One thing that Bush did effectively was consolidate the religious vote, particularly that of evangelicals, and he did so in a manner that provided him with a solid base of support (Himmelfarb, 2001). Further, those evangelicals were eager for a new hero. They had been largely overlooked by Republicans since the 1980 election. Even then, evangelical voters concentrated on senate candidates while listening to the preaching and teaching of ministers such as Jerry Falwell and his Moral Majority. But the influence of the Moral Majority had waned, replaced by a new breed of leaders such as James Dobson and his group, Focus on the Family. Still, Bush "worked hard to court the conservatives and the evangelicals" (Mann & Schlesinger, 2015, 29).

They found their new hero in George W. Bush. The Republican candidate was an ideal person for their support. He admitted to being a reprobate during his younger years, but credited Christianity with turning his life around. In 1980, their support for Ronald Reagan had been constant but tepid; they voted for him, but they didn't like that Reagan was only mildly committed to the Christian religion. His speeches were littered with references to God, but he rarely attended church or espoused beliefs about his personal views on religion. The younger Bush was just the opposite. Not only was he an active Christian, but he truly belonged to their ideal doctrine of a "born-again" Christian. He credited his entire shift in lifestyle to his faith in Jesus. This was a man that evangelicals could support and who would get their votes (Niebuhr, 2000). As Smith (2016) wrote, his "embrace of evangelical Christianity helped anchor him in the fundamentalist culture" (p. xx).

Evangelicals expected a lot from George W. Bush once he was named the winner of the election (Tumulty, et al., 2005). And, for the most part, he came through (Falk, 2006). Evangelical support for Bush influenced at least some of his policy decisions, such as his plan to fight AIDS in Africa (Dyer, 2014). Many of his major appointments went to other evangelicals (Ribuffo, 2006). In fact, Berggren and Rae (2006) compared Bush's presidential style to that of a Democrat, the faith-driven Jimmy Carter. Indeed, President Bush went to great lengths to maintain a positive relationship with broadcast evangelists after his election ("Bush renews ties . . . ", 2003), many of whom had supported his campaign (Sanderbrand, 2004).

And there were other dissenters. One Republican consultant argued that Bush's evangelical strategy led to a divided nation (Janofsky, 2004). However, they were in the minority. In fact, Bush demonstrated that religion could be a major factor in presidential campaigns. He had such strong support from most evangelicals that it actually increased when he ran for re-election in 2004 and was likely the reason he won a majority of the vote that year (Baliner, 2004; "Evangelical Bush," 2005). Indeed, by the end of his terms as president, George W. Bush had effectively demonstrated that evangelical Christians were on the side of the Republicans.

THE THIRD-PARTY CANDIDATE

The fact that there was a major third-party candidate in the 2000 election is often overlooked, but that candidate likely had an effect on the election. Ralph Nader's political appeal came mostly from urban areas and from college-educated voters. Nader failed to get the five percent of the vote that was his campaign goal, but his support in some urban areas was still significant (Hochschild & Wallace, 2011). Nader entered the campaign under the mistaken notion that he would draw support away from Bush, but the opposite happened; his support came almost totally from people who would have voted Democratic otherwise (Nichols, 2004). As a result, his support cut into the popular margin that could have sealed a victory for Al Gore. Many liberals, in fact, attributed Gore's defeat to Nader's entry in the race (Whitmore, 2008), a position supported by subsequent research (Magee, 2003).

THE SUPREME COURT DECIDES

It all came down to Florida. The election was so close that the networks had trouble projecting an early winner in the contest. That changed when exit polling provided by the Voting News Service indicated that Gore would win the state because of strong support in south Florida (Biemer, et al., 2003). Winning Florida provided Gore with enough electoral votes that some television networks started naming him the winner. But the actual vote totals from Florida seemed to cast doubt on that projection. When the final numbers came in, the vote was so close that it triggered an automatic recount. The problem, it turned out, lay in confusion over the "butterfly" computer ballots used in South Florida, particularly in Palm Beach County (Toobin, 2001). This punch-card ballot started with George W. Bush, with the punch spot to the right of his name. Next came the spot for Pat Buchanan, with his name on the opposite side of the ballot but with his punchhole directly under that of Bush's. Gore's name appeared below that of Bush, on the left side of the ballot, with his punchhole being the third in line on the ballot.

What happened is that many new voters, who were heavily Democratic in that area, had mistakenly punched votes for both Al Gore and independent Pat Buchanan, resulting in those ballots being tossed out of the final tally. Or, they simply voted for Buchanan, thinking they were voting for Gore. When the problem became well known, it triggered talk of lawsuits by some Democratic lawyers (Toobin, 2001).

Meanwhile, while most of the media attention was on south Florida, there were also issues regarding the vote totals of black voters in the state, particularly in the city of Jacksonville (Hines, 2002). As Toobin (2001) wrote, "There were reports that Duval County, which included Jacksonville, had an especially high number of under votes in African-American neighborhoods. Could Gore really walk away from this many potential voters?" (39).

Once it was obvious that the results of the election were in doubt, both candidates returned to campaign mode. That was a risky move for Gore, since he could "be branded a sore loser" (Toobin, 2001, 35). Somewhat surprisingly, both used similar arguments about patriotism and democracy to make the case that they should be declared the winner (Isaacson & Chung, 2004). Gore, though, was in the weakest position. As Toobin wrote, "even if the Vice President's team could establish that the butterfly ballot was improper, it was by no means clear that a lawsuit in Palm Beach could propel Gore to the presidency" (35).

Eventually, the Supreme Court entered the controversy; while the Court did not actually name Bush the winner, it ruled in a 5–4 mostly partisan decision that the vote recount in Florida should be halted. Pragmatically, that decision meant that Bush would win (Choper, 2001).

How important was the Supreme Court decision? Extremely. Subsequent research found that Gore would have won the election had it not been for the confusion over the butterfly ballots used in South Florida (Wu, 2006). Further, the result was not all positive for Bush. Bai (2001) noted that Bush's presidency was undermined by the perception that he had won on a "technicality." Cohn (2001) noted that the nature of Bush's win made it harder for him to achieve bipartisan support in Congress, writing that "it's not Democrats who are dwelling on Bush's legal right to be president; it's Republicans. And for good reason" (25).

CONCLUSIONS

Having an election decided by a partisan vote in the Supreme Court is not a way to lessen partisan brinkmanship. In fact, it made things worse by increasing the finger-pointing and blame for the debacle. As Choper (2001) wrote, the decision resulted in "widespread perceptions of partisanship" by the Court (341). In addition, there was a dramatic decline in political trust by the electorate, particularly by black voters (Avery, 2007). Similarly, McGlennon (2001) felt that the decision had an impact on the political stability of the nation.

Although conflict in the Supreme Court occurs behind closed doors, there were signs that the decision had caused problems there, too. The 5–4 decision, with justices casting their ballots mostly along party lines, seemed to increase conflict. That perception became such a problem that in 2016, when Justice Antonin Scalia died unexpectedly, Republicans in the Senate refused to consider the confirmation of President Obama's nominee. Their resistance was based on the hope that Republican Donald Trump could win the presidential election, thus allowing for a Republican to name the new justice and retaining the 5–4 conservative advantage among its members (Herszenhorn & Hulse, 2016).

Even worse, Bush's eight years in the White House only increased tensions between the two parties. Partisan polarization increased significantly following the election (Hadley & Grimmer, 2005). Part of the problem was that Bush entered the presidency with the perception that he had an ideological mandate from the people and that he was the instrument of God in the White House (Smith, 2016). The result, according to Smith, was "Rarely in the history of the United States has the nation been so ill-served as during the presidency of George W. Bush" (xv). By then, of course, both parties were blaming the other for the resulting gridlock.

REFERENCES

Arthos, J. (2002). Appeal to proportion in the Clinton impeachment trial: Reconciling judgment with disposition. *Western Journal of Communication, 66,* 208–228.

Avery, J. (2007). Race, partisanship, and political trust following Bush versus Gore (2000). *Political Behavior, 29,* 327–342.

Bai, M. (2001, August 13). In memory of the lost ballots. *Newsweek, 138(7),* 24–25.

Baliner, R. (2004, July 6). Kerry & the evangelicals. *Nation, 279(1),* 6–8.

Berggren, D. J.. & Rae, N. C. (2006). Jimmy Carter and George W. Bush: Faith, foreign policy and an evangelical presidential style. *Presidential Studies Quarterly, 36(4),* 606–332.

Berman, A. (2015, August 17). The voting-rights counterrevolution. *Nation, 301(7/8),* 16–22.

Biemer, P., Folsom, R., Kulka, R., Lessler, J., Shah, B., & Weeks, M. (2003). An evaluation of procedures and operations used by the Voter News Service for the 2000 presidential election. *Public Opinion Quarterly, 67,* 31–44.

Blow, C. M. (2016, May 9). G.O.P. has only itself to blame. *New York Times,* A19.

Bumiller, E. (2008, January 17). McCain parries a reprise of '00 smear tactics. *New York Times,* A1, A20.

Bush renews ties with television evangelists (2003, March). *Church & State, 58(3),* 16–17.

Choper, J. H. (2001). Why the Supreme Court should not have decided the presidential election of 2000. *Constitutional Commentary, 18,* 335–357.

Cohn, J. (2001, January 29). Loser take all? *New Republic, 224(5),* 24–26.

Cohn, N. (2016, June 30). How Trump could redraw voters' allegiances. *New York Times,* A3.

Dyer, J. H. (2014). The politics of evangelicals: How the issues of HIV and AIDS in Africa shaped a 'centrist' constituency in the United States. *Journal of the American Academy of Religion, 83(4),* 1018–1032.

Evangelical Bush (2005, May 23). *National Review, 57(9),* 59.

Falk, R. (2006). The Christian resurgence and world order. *Brown Journal of World Affairs, 12(2),* 129–137.

Hadley, D. J., & Grimmer, J. R. (2005). *Polarization and depolarization in the 2000 presidential election.* Paper presented at the annual meeting of the Midwestern Political Science Association.

Herszenhorn, D. M., & Hulse, C. (2016, February 26). G.O.P. doubts electoral fallout on court fight. *New York Times*, A1, A3.

Himmelfarb, G. (2001). Religion in the 2000 election. *Public Interest, 143*, 20.

Hines, R. I. (2002). The silent voices: 2000 presidential election and the minority vote in Florida. *Western Journal of Black Studies, 26(2)*, 71–74.

Hochschild, T. R., & Wallace, M. (2011). Three's a crowd? The Nader vote in the 2000 presidential, election in U.S. metropolitan areas. *Social Science Journal, 48*, 575–588.

Howard, L., Gordon, D., Meadows, S., & Begun, B. (2000, June 19). Soft money, hardball tactics. *Newsweek, 135(25)*, 4.

Isaacson, F., & Chung, J. (2004). The Bush vs. Gore rhetoric after the 2000 electoral impasse: A Ch'i-Shih analysis. *Simile, 4(2)*.

Janofsky, M. (2004, November 11). G.O.P. adviser says Bush's evangelical strategy split country. *New York Times*, A23.

Kitchens, J. T., & Powell, L. (1999). Gender and income as factors associated with exposure to jokes about the Clinton–Lewinsky controversy. *Psychological Reports, 84* (1999), 1047–1050.

Magee, C. S. (2003). Third-party candidates and the 2000 presidential election. *Social Science Quarterly, 84*, 574–595.

Mann, J., & Schlesinger, A. M. (2015). *George W. Bush: The 43rd president, 2001–2009*. New York: Henry Holt.

McGlennon, J. J. (2001). The US presidential election of 7 November 2000: What happens when a nation can't decide. *Australian Journal of Political Science, 36*, 157–162.

Nichols, J. (2004, November 15). Nader's flawed calculus. *Nation, 279(16)*, 28.

Niebuhr, G. (2000, February 21). Evangelicals found a believer in Bush. *New York Times*, A13.

Piepenburg, E. (2016, July 7). A political monologuist and his summer of Trump. *New York Times*, C1, C6.

Ribuffo, L. (2006). George W. Bush and the latest evangelical menace. *Dissent, 53(4)*, 42–49.

Sanderbrand, R. (2004, November 1). Shepherding the flock. *Newsweek, 144(18)*, 26.

Sheppard, S. (2013). Race, class, and values in post-New Deal presidential politics: Inverted class loyalties as a trend in presidential elections, 2000–2012. *New Political Science, 35*, 272–306.

Silva, C. L., Jenkins-Smith, H. C., & Waterman, R. (2007). Why did Clinton survive the impeachment process? A test of three explanations. *Presidential Studies Quarterly, 37*, 468–485.

Smith, J. E. (2016). *Bush*. New York: Simon & Schuster.

Toobin, J. (2001). *Too close to call: The thirty-six day battle to decide the 2000 election*. New York: Random House.

Tumulty, K., Cooper, M., Calabresi, M., & Healy, R. (2005, February 7). What does Bush owe the religious right? *Time, 165(6)*, 28–32.

Whitmore, A. (2008). Schism on the left: The motivations and impact of Ralph Nader's candidacy. *Political Quarterly, 79*, 566–569.

Wu, D. W. (2006). Who should be the winner? A post hoc analysis of the 2000 US election. *International Journal of Mathematical Education in Science and Technology, 37(1)*, 81–87.

NINE

2008: Obama, Hope, and Reform

Despite barely winning his 2000 election, George W. Bush easily won his re-election campaign in 2004. Bush was aided by a weak opponent in Democrat John Kerry plus a nasty and false negative campaign run by a group that called themselves the "Swift Boat Veterans." The essence of their campaign was that Kerry received medals he never deserved for battles that were never fought. Bush himself was reluctant to disavow the group's ads. Ultimately, the ads of the Swift Boat Veterans turned out to be full of lies. As Rutenberg and Bosman wrote, "One of [the accusers] had earned a medal for bravery in a gun battle he accused Mr. Kerry of concocting" (A14). But the truth didn't come out until after the election. By then, another brick had been laid into the "anything goes" form of campaigning, i.e., a candidate could and would say anything about an opponent (even if it was obviously false) if it would help in the campaign.

As Bush's second term approached its end, Democrats were emboldened by the prospect of regaining the White House. After all, Bush enacted tax cuts early in his first term that had ruined Clinton's balanced budgets. The trickle-down effect that Bush expected tax cuts to trigger never happened, leaving the nation in debt. By the end of the Bush era, that debt was mounting quickly.

Meanwhile, the Iraq War was entering its fifth year, and Bush showed no intention of backing off his commitment there (Myers, 2008), nor was their much hope of ending it soon (O'Hanlon, 2008). At the same time, many voters had concerns about the nation's economy, which seemed to be working against the middle class (Sussman, 2007; Leonhardt, 2007; Krugman, 2008), mainly due to the rapidly rising cost of oil and gas (Healey & Hagenbaugh, 2008) and high mortgage rates (Kiely & Page, 2008). And for the Democrats, health care became a major issue (Leibovich, 2007).

Up stepped some Democrats who thought that the health issue would give them an edge in the approaching election. The biggest name associated with the issue was Hillary Clinton, who saw the election as an opportunity for her to become the nation's first woman president. Her strongest challenger was a young, first-term African-American senator from Illinois named Barack Obama. He offered a message of hope that led him to an upset win in Iowa (Nagourney, 2008, January 4) and that would eventually carry him to the White House. Other candidates included Connecticut senator Christopher Dodd, New Mexico governor Bill Richardson, Delaware senator Joe Biden, former Alaska senator Mike Gravel, and Ohio representative Dennis J. Kucinich (Steinberg & Hernandez, 2007).

As the Democratic contests continued, Obama shocked many observers by his ability to raise money. By March, Obama had raised more than $90 million.

The nation's racists were shocked when a black man won the Democratic nomination. Republicans generally did not expect to lose the election, but their confidence was badly shaken when Barack Obama easily won the general election. What followed were a series of racially based attacks on the new president, ranging from claims that he was a Muslim to questions about whether he was truly a natural-born citizen of the United States. Those racial attacks continued for much of his presidency.

THE PRIMARIES

Hillary Clinton looked like the favorite prior to any of the Democratic primaries. That perception was badly shaken when Obama won the Iowa caucuses. Meanwhile, former North Carolina senator John Edwards appeared to be a major candidate as well (Bosman, 2008, March 21), although he eventually fell behind and later had to face an admission of adultery exposed while he was campaigning (Moore, 2008).

While racism would be covertly apparent in the general election, the problem first appeared in the Democratic primaries. Some supporters of Hillary Clinton made some racial remarks that were obviously aimed at Obama (Healy & Zeleny, 2008; Purnick, 2008). Meanwhile, as the Democratic primaries continued with no obvious winner emerging, the party faithful became concerned that a long campaign could hurt their chances of success in November (Nagourney & Zeleny, 2008). A Gallup poll, indeed, found that many of Obama's supporters would not vote for Clinton, and many Clinton supporters had a similar opinion of Obama (Seelye, 2008, March 27).

Meanwhile, the Republicans had both Mitt Romney and John McCain hoping to replace Bush in the White House. Romney raised and spent the most money, more than $100 million (Wayne, 2008, March 7). Others in the race included former Speaker of the House Newt Gingrich and former Arkansas governor Mike Huckabee. The winner, though, was McCain. By early March, he had sewed up his claim to the Republican position while the Democrats still seemed to be in disarray (Nagourney, 2008, March 5).

That situation started to change in late March when Clinton's campaign stalled and Obama's hope campaign took control (Brooks, 2008, March 25). The major momentum shift came after Clinton inaccurately spoke of coming under enemy fire while landing in Bosnia in 1996 (Healy & Seelye, 2008). As Rich (2008, March 30) questioned, "Why did she keep repeating this whopper for nearly three months, well after it had been publicly debunked by journalists and eyewitnesses?" (WK13).

Eventually, the race boiled down to Obama versus McCain. A potential preview of the race arose in a test case in Illinois in March when a special election was held to elect a replacement for former Republican Speaker of the House Dennis Hastert. The victory by the Democrats there buoyed their hopes that they could win the presidency (Hulse, 2008).

THE GENERAL ELECTION AND MONEY

After the conventions of both parties had settled, the race became one of the youth of Barack Obama and the experience of John McCain. Obama was highly articulate and his oratorical skills far outshined those of McCain. But he also had another advantage—a better-financed campaign.

McCain would be the last major presidential nominee to use federal funds to finance his campaign. And, the Republican nominee had a vested interest in doing so; he was, after all, the co-sponsor of the legislation that authorized those federal funds while trying to limit how much candidates could spend. The McCain–Feingold campaign finance reform bill was officially called the "Bipartisan Campaign Reform Act of 1997," but it was more commonly known as simply the McCain–Feingold bill. Further, it reflected a basic goal for the senator from Arizona to try to reduce the impact that money had on elections. Thus he had a great deal of personal motivation for complying with its legal premises, given that he was the Republican nominee. Unfortunately for McCain, he seemed to have forgotten that "In politics, money is always the driving force" (Smith, et al., 2009, 8). Thus, he accepted the provisions of his own law and the restrictions that they presented.

Obama was under no such restriction; indeed, he had already demonstrated an ability to raise vast amounts of money during the primaries. Thus he declined to accept any federal funds and financed his entire campaign using donations from the public. By early August, the Obama campaign had amassed a war chest of more than $340 million, with half of that coming from donations of $200 or less (Luo & Drew, 2008). McCain, by comparison, raised only $27 million during the month of July ("McCain raised . . . , 2008). Once McCain officially received the Republican nomination, though, he got an immediate infusion of $84 million (Luo & Zeleny, 2008). Unfortunately for McCain, that would be all that he would ever get from the presidential campaign fund. And, while that figure looked impressive at the time, it ended up being no match for the funds that Obama was able to raise. Obama raised $69 million in September alone, with his total donor base reaching more than three million people (Luo, 2008).

The additional funds allowed Obama to engage in organizational approaches in five swing states that were beyond the reach of the McCain campaign. In Ohio, for example, the Obama campaign divided the state into 1,231 targeted neighborhoods. Information, including voting history, on each area was obtained from a variety of data sources, "including magazine subscriptions, the types of cars people drive, where voters shop, and how much they earn." Each name was bar-coded and provided to teams of volunteers, who then contacted each individual by telephone or by knocking on their doors. "And each of these teams, if the recruiting is up to speed, has a leader who, ideally, lives just down the block from all those doors that need to be knocked on" (Zeleny, 2008, A22). As Wayne (2008, November 1) later wrote, "By investing heavily in microtargeting, the [Obama] campaign has built a ground game that has helped put more closely contested states into play and forced the Republicans to compete in states they have handily won in the past" (A15).

Obama would eventually raise about $750 million for his entire campaign, a new record in presidential campaign funds. In addition, Obama also had enough extra money to pay for a 30-minute infomercial late in October that was broadcast live on NBC, CBS, Fox, Univision, BET, and TV One (Rutenberg, 2008, October 29). By then, the McCain campaign was nearly broke and was "running on a shoestring and conviction" (Bosman, 2008, October 29, A21).

MCCAIN AND SARAH PALIN

Not only was McCain hurt by lack of money, but he also took a gamble on his vice presidential pick. His naming of Alaska governor Sarah Palin as his running mate was a "Hail Mary" selection that he hoped would give him a chance in the presidential ball game. Initially, her selection was well received, particularly by the party faithful. As conservative columnist David Brooks of the *New York Times* (2008, September 5) wrote, "She gave a tough vice-presidential speech. . . . And what was most impressive was her speech's freshness . . . her language resonated more of supermarket aisle than the megachurch pulpit" (A27). Similarly,

William Kristol (2008) noted that her speech had made her the center of attention in the election and openly asked whether "a star is born" (A21), while President George W. Bush described her selection as an "inspired pick" (quoted by Phillips, 2008, A21). Further, McCain's selection did seem successful in energizing the convention crowd (Bumiller & Cooper, 2008) and in galvanizing the Republican base (Kirkpatrick, 2008). She drew strong crowds for the candidate in their joint appearances (Bumiller, 2008). And her strong religious views made her particularly popular with the religious right (Johnson & Severson, 2008).

That freshness, though, quickly evaporated. As Herbert (2008, September 6) wrote, "Sarah Palin may someday become president, and for all we know she may be a great one. But she was not chosen as Mr. McCain's running mate after long and careful consideration and consultation. The best evidence is that she was a somewhat impulsive choice" (A23). And while she helped to solidify the Republican base, her views merely increased the polarization of the rest of the voters. As Collins (2008) wrote, "her supporters re-ignited the cultural wars we thought might lay at least semi-dormant this season" (A27).

Instead, Palin's selection became the subject of jokes and ridicule, particularly as portrayed on *Saturday Night Live* by comic actress Tina Fey (Fairbanks, 2008). As the ridicule mounted, concerned campaign aides worked to prepare Palin for a serious interview on issues (Rutenberg & Davey, 2008). The effort was only partially successful, with Palin appearing visibly nervous and unprepared. In response to a question about whether she agreed with the Bush policy against terrorism, for example, "Ms. Palin did not seem to know what she was talking about" (Rutenberg, 2008, September 12, A17). That exchange was one reason that commentator Charles Blow (2008) wrote that "Palin could become a liability for McCain," adding, "It turns out that the Republican enthusiasm for Sarah Palin is just as superficial as she is . . . on the issues, even they worry about her" (A31).

In an attempt to alleviate the problem, the McCain campaign scheduled a second interview for Palin, this time with Katie Couric of CBS. It didn't help; in fact, it was arguably worse than the first one. As TV reviewer Alessandra Stanley (2008) wrote regarding Palin's response to a question about Russia, "Palin's answer was surprisingly wobbly; her words tumbled out fast and choppily, like an outboard motor loosened from the stern." And, Stanley added, "That exchange was so startling it ricocheted across the Internet several hours before it appeared on CBS" (A20). After that, even some Republicans had doubts about her ability to serve as vice president (Nagourney, 2008, September 30). That impression increased further when, during the vice presidential debate, Palin was unable to name a single Supreme Court case other than *Roe vs. Wade* (Seelye, 2008, October 2). Later, she was stumped by a question from a third-grade student who asked her about the duties of the vice president, leading Egan (2008) to write, "Whether Americans are real or fake, they can see through Palin, a woman" (WK14).

Eventually, Palin started using the rhetoric of victimization, blaming the media for her problems (Powell & Hickson, 2014). Still, she accentuated one problem that would continue through the next two presidential elections—class warfare. As David Brooks (2008, October 10) wrote, Republicans entered the 2008 election with a history of targeting rural voters, while simultaneously alienating educated and urban voters. Palin touched that nerve and emphasized it even more. By the end of the campaign, Sarah Palin was hurting John McCain, not helping him (Cooper, 2008, October 31).

THE GENERAL ELECTION AND RACISM

Once Obama had the Democratic nomination, Matt Bai (2008) pondered the question, "Is Obama the end of black politics?" (34). History would say the answer was an emphatic "No." Quite the contrary, Obama's presence in the campaign, and even more so during his eventual win, brought out latent racism from some of his opponents.

In fact, the racial attacks against Obama were in full bloom by August. The biggest bullet came from a conspiracy writer named Jerome Corsi (2008), whose book, *Where's the Birth Certificate?* reached No. 1 on the *New York Times* best-seller list, (1) raised doubts about Obama being an American citizen and (2) raised claims that he was actually a Muslim. Those two arguments would haunt Obama during the entire campaign and through both terms of his presidency. The fact that he was actually a native-born American citizen, born in Hawaii, and that he was an active Christian seemed irrelevant to his critics. Rutenberg and Bosman (2008) noted that the charges were levied with the same intent that the false attacks of the Swift Boat Veterans had had on John Kerry, i.e., destroy Obama's credibility with the voters. Thus they concluded that the charges attempted to define him "as a stealth radical liberal who has tried to cover up 'extensive connections to Islam'" (A1).

Herbert (2008, August 2) described the attack as a covert argument aimed to undercut Obama's support because he was an African-American. Kristof (2008) noted that the goal of the campaign was to argue that Obama was a Muslim and perhaps even the Antichrist. And Kristof added, "To his credit, Mr. McCain himself has never raised doubts about Mr. Obama's religion. But a McCain commercial last month mimicked the words and imagery of the best-selling 'Left Behind' book series in ways that would have set off alarm bells among evangelicals nervous about the Antichrist." Further, Kristol concluded, "religious prejudice is becoming a proxy for racial prejudice. In public at least, it's not acceptable to express reservations about a candidate's skin color, so discomfort about race is sublimated into concerns about whether Mr. Obama is sufficiently Christian" (WK9).

That issue invariably led to the next charge: a claim by John McCain himself. In August, McCain openly complained that Obama was using the "race card" to increase his support among voters. Obama, mentioning some of the attacks levied against him, told his supporters that Republicans would try to scare voters by pointing out he "doesn't look like all those other presidents on the dollar bills." McCain's campaign manager countered by saying that "Barack Obama has played the race card, and he played it from the bottom of the deck." McCain later agreed, saying, "It's divisive, negative, shameful and wrong." (Cooper & Powell, 2008, A1).

Later, the McCain campaign ran an ad that featured Britney Spears and Paris Hilton in the opening. The ad was critical of Obama. Herbert (2008, August 2) noted that the ad was "designed to exploit the hostility, anxiety and resentment of the many white Americans who are still freakishly hung up on the idea of black men rising above their station and becoming sexually involved with white women." And, he added, "It is driving the idea that Barack Obama is somehow presumptuous, too arrogant, too big for his britches—a man who obviously does not know his place" (A27).

Toward the end of the campaign, as Obama's lead increased so did the racial attacks. They had shifted, though, into criticism that Obama was not just a Muslim but also a terrorist. As Frank Rich (2008, October 12) wrote, "By the time McCain asks the crowd 'Who is the real Barack Obama?' it's no surprise that someone cries out 'Terrorist!'" And, he added, "This sleight of hand at once synchronizes with the poisonous Obama-is-a-Muslim e-mail blasts and shifts the brand of terrorism . . . to the radical Islamic threats of today" (WK10). That charge was followed by a claim from a man named Andy Martin who argued that Obama was a radical Muslim. Martin put out a press release two weeks after Obama spoke at the 2004 Democratic Convention. "Obama is a Muslim who has concealed his religion," he wrote and said on Fox News. As Rutenberg (2008, October 13) noted, "The Fox program allowed Mr. Martin to assert falsely and without challenge that Mr. Obama had once trained to overthrow the government" (A1).

As the campaign continued through mid-October, race remained a covert issue. The Republican attack machine did not overtly refer to Obama's racial heritage, but it frequently used the term that he was "not one of us" (quoted by Healy, 2008, A16). As Healy added, "race has erupted as an issue mostly in ways that seem to confirm how deep the divide remains for some voters—those expressing mistrust over Mr. Obama's ties to his controversial pastor . . . or those describing Mr. Obama as 'uppity' or 'elitist.'" The attacks seemed to be particularly effective in the

South where, as Nossiter (2008) wrote, the racial issues "found a recep-
tive audience with many white Southern voters" (A21).

Eventually, though, the racial overtones did not work, and the voters
sided with Obama (Cooper & Thee, 2008). By the time they did, most
observers had too. As Herbert (2008) wrote, "Senator Obama has spoken
more honestly and thoughtfully about race than any other politician in
many years. Senator McCain is the head of a party that has viciously
exploited race for political gain for decades" (A27). Similarly, Frank Rich
wrote, "Obama doesn't transcend race. He isn't post-race. He is the latest
chapter in the ever-furling American racial saga . . . we turned to the
black guy not only because we hoped he would lift us up but because he
looked like the strongest leader to dig us out" (WK10).

THE COLLAPSE OF THE BANKING INDUSTRY

Perhaps the final nail in McCain's chances of winning came when the
banking industry collapsed. The first warning of economic troubles came
in early September when the U.S. stock market suffered its worst loss
since 2001 (Calmes, 2008), followed by rising unemployment (Uchitelle,
2008). Then the federal government had to bail out its two biggest mortgage programs, Fannie Mae and Freddie Mac (Labaton & Sorkin, 2008).
Eventually, the banking problems spread to other institutions and required more federal intervention and forcing responses from both candidates (Cooper, 2008, September 25). Stolberg (2008) described the time
following the collapse as "days of chaos" (A1).

McCain ended up being the loser on the exchange, partly because he
cancelled an appearance on the *The Late Show with David Letterman* because of the crisis, but then did an interview for CBS News at the same
time that he would have been on "Letterman." As Carter (2008) wrote,
Letterman "was so unhappy that Mr. McCain canceled his scheduled
'Late Show' appearance that he spent much of the first segment assailing
the senator's decision" (A22). McCain eventually made a follow-up appearance on the show, where he apologized and said "I screwed up"
(Stetler, 2008, A19).

Eventually, the public went with Obama again. In a national poll con-
ducted in early October, Obama had taken a nine-point lead over McCain
based on how they each handled the crisis (Nagourney & Thee, 2008).
Late in the month, even conservative commentators were predicting an
Obama win. David Brooks (2008, October 26), for example, concluded,
"McCain would be an outstanding president. . . . But he never escaped
the straightjacket of a party that is ailing and a conservatism that is behind the times. And that's what makes the final weeks of this campaign
so unspeakably sad" (WK14).

Indeed, as the campaign approached the final days, the banking industry and the economy emerged as the dominant issues (Baker & Zeleny, 2008). That wasn't good news for John McCain.

CONCLUSIONS

The 2008 election focused on money, racism, and a broken economy. Each of those factors would reappear in the future. In particular, the pillars of fear (the argument behind racism) and consumerism (the economy) would resurface during the 2012 election when Obama ran for re-election. Perhaps of more importance was the shape of the Republican Party following the election. From 1968 through 2004, Republicans had won seven of ten presidential elections. But that changed in 2008 with Barack Obama. As Tanenhaus (2008) wrote, after the election, the Republican Party was "now full of questions and without a center" (P1) and "Sectarian rifts threaten a coalition once noted for unity" (P9).

Perhaps no other event increased the attribution of blame more than the presence of a black man in the White House. Republicans seemed to take offense at the idea, hurling attack after attack in the direction of the president. He was criticized (falsely) as being an illegitimate president because he had not been born in the United States. Others complained that he was secretly a Muslim who sided with terrorists. Democrats, meanwhile, came to his defense with an equal level of fervor. The result was a classic example of Berne's transactional analysis. Both sides adopted the parent role in the interaction, talking as if the other side was a petulant child. The result was the crossed lines that Berne said typified unsuccessful conflict, i.e., both sides taking the parental role, addressing the other as a child, and neither side entering the debate from the perspective of an adult.

REFERENCES

Bai, M. (2008, August 10). What would a black president mean for black politics? *New York Times Magazine*, 34–41, 50, 54–55.

Baker, P., & Zeleny, J. (2008, October 30). In final rounds of appeals, the economy dominates. *New York Times*, A25.

Blow, C. M. (2008, September 20). Lipstick bungle. *New York Times*, A31.

Bosman, J. (2008, March 21). Edwards on Leno. *New York Times*, A16.

Bosman, J. (2008, October 29). On campuses, McCain supporters are running on a shoestring and conviction. *New York Times*, A21.

Brooks, D. (2008, March 25). The long defeat. *New York Times*, A27.

Brooks, D. (2008, September 5). A glimpse of the new. *New York Times*, A27.

Brooks, D. (2008, October 10). The class war before Palin. *New York Times*, A29.

Brooks, D. (2008, October 26). Ceding the center. *New York Times*, WK14.

Bumiller, E. (2008, September 11). With Palin at his side, McCain finds energized crowds. *New York Times*, A19.

Bumiller, E., & Cooper, M. (2008, September 4). Palin takes center stage for enthusiastic G.O.P. *New York Times*, A1, A21.

Calmes, J. (2008, September 16). Wall St. in worst loss since '01 despite reassurances by Bush. *New York Times*, A1, A22.

Carter, B. (2008, September 25). Letterman, spurned. *New York Times*, A22.

Collins, G. (2008, September 4). Sarah Palin speaks! *New York Times*, A27.

Cooper, M. (2008, September 25). For both nominees, new roles and new risks. *New York Times*, A22.

Cooper, M. (2008, October 31). Growing doubts on Palin take a toll, poll finds. *New York Times*, A1, A18.

Cooper, M., & Powell, M. (2008, August 1). McCain camp says Obama plays 'race card.' *New York Times*, A1, A14.

Cooper, M., & Thee, M. (2008, October 15). Poll says McCain is hurting his bid by using attacks. *New York Times*, A1.

Corsi, J. (2008). *Where's the birth certificate?: The case that Barack Obama is not eligible to be president*. Washington, DC: WND Books.

Egan, T. (2008, October 26). The party of yesterday. *New York Times*, WK14.

Fairbanks, A. M. (2008, September16). Finding her inner Palin. *New York Times*, A21.

Healey, J. R., & Hagenbaugh, B. (2008, March 11). Record fuel prices blow budgets. *USA Today*, 1B-2B.

Healy, (2008, October 13). Race remains campaign issue, but not a clear one. *New York Times*, A16.

Healy, P., & Seelye, K. Q. (2008, March 25). Clinton says she 'misspoke' about dodging sniper fire. *New York Times*, A16.

Healy, P., & Zeleny, J. (2008, March 13). Racial issue bubbles up again for Democrats. *New York Times*, A1, A14.

Herbert, B. (2008, August 2). Running while black. *New York Times*, A27.

Herbert, B. (2008, September 6). Running from reality. *New York Times*, A23.

Hulse, C. (2008, March 10). Democrats confident after taking G.O.P. seat in Illinois. *New York Times*, A11.

Johnson, K., & Severson, K. (2008, September 6). In Palin's worship and politics a desire to follow God's will. *New York Times*, A1, A12.

Kiely, K., & Page, S. (2008, March 28). Obama, Clinton offer plans for mortgage help, jobs retraining. *USA Today*, 5A.

Kirkpatrick, D. D. (2008, September 3). Wooing conservatives pays off. *New York Times*, A1, A14.

Kristof, N. D. (2008, September 21). The push to 'otherize' Obama. *New York Times*, WK9.

Kristol, W. (2008, September 1). A star is born? *New York Times*, A21.

Krugman, (2008, March 7). The anxiety election. *New York Times*, A19.

Labaton, S., & Sorkin, A. R. (2008, September 6). U.S. rescue seen at hand for two mortgage giants. *New York Times*, A1, B8.

Leibovich, M. (2007, February 18). Leftward, ho? *New York Times*, 4–1, 4–4.

Leonhardt, D. (2007, December 30). Polls indicate voter anxiety over economy. *New York Times*, A15.

Luo, M. (2008, October 20). Obama's September success recasts the campaign fundraising landscape. *New York Times*, A21.

Luo, M., & Drew, C. (2008, August 6). Big donors, too, have seats at Obama fundraising table. *New York Times*, A1, A16.

Luo, M., & Zeleny, J. (2008, September 9). Minus U.S. money, Obama team presses donors. *New York Times*, A1, A20.

McCain raised $27 million in July (2008, August 16). *New York Times*, A12.

Moore, S. (2008, August 9). Edwards admits to affair in 2006. *New York Times*, A1, A12.

Myers, S. L. (2008, March 20). Marking 5 years, Bush insists U.S. must win in Iraq. *New York Times*, A1, A11.

Nagourney, A. (2008, January. 4). Obama triumphs in Iowa contest; Huckabee rolls. *New York Times*, A1, A13.

Nagourney, A. (2008, March 5). McCain claims nomination as Democrats duel. *New York Times*, A1, A17.

Nagourney, A. (2008, September 30). Concerns about Palin's readiness as a big test for her nears. *New York Times*, A16.

Nagourney, A., & Thee, M. (2008, October 2). Poll finds Obama gaining support and McCain weakened in bailout crisis. *New York Times*, A23.

Nagourney, A., & Zeleny, J. (2008, March 16). For Democrats, increased fears of a long fight. *New York Times*, A1, A22.

Nossiter, A. (2008, October 15). For some, uncertainty starts at racial identity. *New York Times*, A21.

O'Hanlon, M. (2008, March 11). Reality and the Iraq war. *USA Today*, 11A.

Phillips, K. (2008, September 9). . . . But an 'inspired pick.' *New York Times*, A21.

Powell, L., & Hickson, M., III (2014). Sarah Palin and the rhetoric of victimage: From pit bull to victim. *Journalism and Mass Communication, 4(1),* 13–25.

Purnick, J. (2008, March 13). Ferraro is unapologetic in leaving post with Clinton campaign. *New York Times*, A14.

Rich, F. (2008, March 30). Hillary's St. Patrick's Day massacre. *New York Times*, WK13.

Rich, F. (2008, October 12). The terrorist Barack Hussein Obama. *New York Times*, WK10.

Rich, F. (2008, November 2). Guess who's coming to dinner. *New York Times*, WK10.

Rutenberg, J. (2008, September 12). In first big interview, Palin says 'I'm ready' for the job. *New York Times*, A1, A17.

Rutenberg, J. (2008, October 13). The man behind the whispers about Obama. *New York Times*, A1, A18.

Rutenberg, J. (2008, October 29). Obama infomercial, a closing argument to everyman. *New York Times*, A18.

Rutenberg, J., & Bosman, J. (2008, August 13). Book attacking Obama hopes to repeat '04 anti-Kerry feat. *New York Times*, A1, A14.

Rutenberg, J., & Davey, M. (2008, September 11). Squad of G.O.P. aides prepares Palin for interviews. *New York Times*, A19.

Seelye, K. Q. (2008, March 27). Leaving Democrats' fold? *New York Times*, A23.

Seelye, K. Q. (2008, October 2). Palin cites no grudge with court; Biden's is personal. *New York Times*, A22.

Smith, M. M., Williams, G. C., Powell, L., & Copeland, G. (2009). *Campaign finance reform: The political shell game.* Lanham, MD: Lexington.

Stanley, A. (2008, September 26). A question reprised in a third Palin interview, but the words come no more easily. *New York Times*, A20.

Steinberg, J., & Hernandez, R. (2007, June 1). 2 more Democratic candidates decline to join in Fox News debate. *New York Times*, A20.

Stelter, B. (2008, October 17). McCain faces Letterman. *New York Times*, A19.

Stolberg, S. G. (2008, September 26). Day of chaos grips Washington; fate of bailout plan unresolved. *New York Times*, A1, A22.

Sussman, D. (2007, November 6). Economy catching up as an issue. *New York Times*, A20.

Tanenhaus, S. (2008, November 6). A once-united G.O.P. emerges, in identity crisis. *New York Times*, P1, P9.

Uchitelle, L. (2008, September 6). U.S. jobless rate climbs past 6%, highest since '03. *New York Times*, A1, A13.

Wayne, L. (2008, March 7). Donations keep pouring in, but for at least one candidate, there's a catch. *New York Times*, A8.

Wayne, L. (2008, November 1). Democrats take page from their rival's playbook. *New York Times*, A15.

Zeleny, J. (2008, October 12). Obama aims for electoral edge, block by block. *New York Times*, A1, A22.

TEN

The 2010 Congressional Elections

A strange thing happened after the 2008 election. All of a sudden, Republicans responded en masse by hating the new president (Bond, 2013). Maybe it was simply because Barack Obama was a Democrat. However, it seemed like a lot of that hatred had to do with his race. The racism that dogged Obama in the 2008 election merely expanded after he was inaugurated as president.

Obama had campaigned on providing a health insurance plan that would cover more people while also pledging to unite the parties. He was able to pass a health-care plan, but barely. He kept holding it back, hoping to get some Republican support for it and thus fulfill both of his pledges at once. When Republican opposition became obstinate, he finally pushed it through Congress without their support. That merely made the Republicans even madder.

That set up the 2010 midterm elections and a lot of angry Republican voters. Those voters became a rather loosely-knit association of individuals who became known as the Tea Party. The Tea Party became a major force in the 2010 election and continued to have an influence through 2014. The Democrats, meanwhile, were counting on support because of an improving economy under President Obama and the number of people who obtained health insurance for the first time under the Affordable Care Act (Stonecash, 2010). As a result, the 2010 election became a true national election, with results at a local or state level that had an impact on the entire nation (Aldrich, et al., 2014). That nationalization was perhaps epitomized when one senator, Arlen Specter, switched parties, leaving the Republicans and becoming a Democrat; Democrats welcomed him, but Republicans viewed it as an opportunistic move to increase his chances for re-election (Evers, Peterson & Hadley, 2012).

Not everyone anticipated the importance of the election. Overall, national turnout was down, compared to the 2008 election, and it was particularly low among young adults (McDonald, 2010). Further, the 2010 elections were the first major campaigns in which social media started playing a role, including the Coffee House posts on Facebook (Mascaro, Novak, & Coggins, 2012). Candidates of the time didn't understand or use the new media at first, not realizing that participants in social media could not be influenced by traditional campaign techniques, such as the use of television ads (Vacarri & Nielsen, 2013).

The Republicans were aided by a new ruling from the U.S. Supreme Court in a case called *Citizens United v. the FEC*. That decision ruled that corporations were people and thus eligible to donate to political campaigns. Later rulings by the court expanded the interpretation to include donations to "Super PACs," i.e., candidates could raise unlimited amounts of money from those donors for outside interest groups as long as those groups did not coordinate their activities with the candidates themselves.

The combination of Tea Party voters and unlimited contributions changed how Republicans campaigned in 2010. Democrats, who were philosophically opposed to the *Citizens United* decision, didn't participate in the Super PAC industry that Republicans ran rampant in 2010 (Smith & Powell, 2013). Democrats feared, even early in the election, that they would face problems at the polls (Cook, 2010). That frame of mind was supported by pre-election polling that found Republicans had an eight percent edge in partisanship (Batum, Erikson, & Wiezien, 2010). The Democrats' pessimism turned out to be correct. The party paid for the decision not to form Super PACs by losing more than its share of elections.

THE TEA PARTY

Most observers believe the Tea Party had a major influence on the 2010 election, and the group definitely intended to have such an impact after the elections (Feldman, 2010). Evaluating the specific nature of that impact was harder to do. As Feldman wrote, "Trying to get a handle on how tea partyers will affect these votes can be like watching cats wrestle under the carpet. You know something's going on, but you're not quite sure what" (N). Still, most observers thought something was happening.

Carson and Pettigrew (2013) were the exception. They argued that the Tea Party had little impact on the 2010 election. But their conclusion was in a definite minority. Instead, most observers felt that the Tea Party revitalized a stunned Republican Party. As Skocpol and Williamson (2012) noted, after the 2008 election, enthusiasm among Democrats was up and that of Republicans down. "With rising cohorts of younger and minority voters energized on behalf of Barack Obama and the Democrats, the crestfallen GOP looked like a relic of the past, fast fading into irrelevance," they wrote (6).

The Tea Party emerged as a reactionary force in American politics early in 2010. Parker (2013) noted that the movement emerged from a fear among those voters that America had changed for the worse. That conclusion is consistent with the Four Pillars model (Kitchens & Powell, 2015), which argues that fear is one of four major factors influencing American politics. Skocpol and Williamson (2012) argue that the group formed on the basis of an even more dubious fear, i.e., racial opposition to President Barack Obama for his "ObamaCare" medical insurance program and his plan to save the American banking industry from the collapse of the mortgage industry. From their viewpoint, Obama was merely moving to save the homes of individuals who could not pay for their own homes.

Aldrich, et al. (2014) noted that Tea Party supporters arose because they (1) blamed Democrats for the problems with government that they disliked, and (2) they opposed the Democrats' legislative agenda. Brown (2010) argued that many Tea Party voters were former supporters of independent candidate Ross Perot, only 18 years older for this election than they were when they supported Perot in 1992. Further, while some Tea Party supporters were independents (Kucera, 2010) who also disliked Republicans (Grunwald & Crowley, 2010), nearly three-fourths were strongly conservative in their political ideology and a majority were angry at the system (Brown, 2010). Brown also noted that the issues that concerned them the most were limiting the role of the federal government, lower taxes, and reducing the federal debt, while social conservative issues (e.g., abortion, gay marriage) were of little concern to them. Thus Kucera (2010) wrote that "the common themes of the Tea Party movement include fiscal responsibility, distrust of big government and abolishing most taxes" (40). In fact, the focus of some Tea Party groups was more on referenda that reduced taxes than on electing conservative candidates (Stone, 2010). In terms of pragmatic impact, that meant voting "for candidates who can displace Barack Obama and other Democrats" (Skocpol & Williamson, 2012, 27).

The philosophy was particularly appealing to the far-right members of the Republican Party (Jacobsen, 2011). In addition, many Tea Party candidates received endorsements and additional support from high-profile Republicans such as former vice-presidential candidate Sarah Palin (Bullock & Hood, 2012). As a result, by the time that voters went to the polls in November, the Tea Party had been gradually pulled into and become an unofficial part of the Republican Party (Courser, 2010).

The roots of the movement started early in 2009, "just weeks into the Obama presidency" (Skocpol & Williamson, 2012, 5).

Carlson (2012) noted that the Tea Party freshmen in Congress "set out to change Washington but settled for simply paralyzing it" (7A). The group tried 33 times to repeal Obama's healthcare plan, with no success. Even the Republican Party was paralyzed. According to Carlson, "[Speaker of the House] Boehner . . . doesn't lead his troops so much as try to keep from being run over by them" (7A).

Regardless, Senior (2010) argued that one lesson of the Tea Party movement was that candidates needed to understand the average voter's sense of vulnerability and their perception of self-importance. And, she predicted, another element of the Tea Party success is that it likely signaled an increase in the role of narcissism in national elections. Both conclusions proved to be accurate and reached new heights during the 2016 presidential election, even though the Tea Party movement itself had largely evaporated by then.

CITIZENS UNITED V. FEC

The way that political campaigns were financed started to change after a ruling by the Supreme Court in the case of *Citizens United v. FEC*. Citizens United was an independent political group that sought to run ads during the 2008 election, only to be stymied by current laws regulating the raising of political money. Their legal existence, at the time, was governed by the FCRA (Federal Campaign Reform Act), a law sometimes referred to as the McCain–Feingold Act, which regulated the raising of campaign-related funds. Those regulations included limits on how much any one individual could contribute to a campaign, and also prohibited corporations from making political contributions. Citizens United sued the Federal Election Commission, arguing that it should be able to raise more money from individuals and corporations and should also be able to contribute to the political process. In a 5–4 decision, the Supreme Court agreed with Citizens United. The result, as Fang (2014) later wrote, was a ruling that provided a guideline for "how to buy an election" (18), while the *Harvard Law Review* argued that it "legalized coercion in the workplace" ("Citizens United at work," 2014, 669). A key element of the decision was that corporations should have the same rights as citizens; that ruling was based on a 1978 case, *First National Bank of Boston v. Bellotti,* and essentially gave corporations the right to donate and spend money in political campaigns (Raskin, 2012). Many questioned the decision (e.g., Chavez, 2011), but objections had few consequences; the ruling remained the law of the land.

The result of the new ruling had major consequences for the 2010 election. First, Democrats philosophically disagreed with the ruling (Smith, 2011). Instead of raising money under the new guidelines, the Democratic Party (and its candidates) simply expressed its displeasure with the decision. Republicans, meanwhile, starting raising money and raising a lot of it. Second, the decision allowed for the creation of a new type of independent group known as the "Super PAC." Super PACs were allowed to raise an unlimited amount of money, with donations coming from rich individuals (who could contribute as much as they wanted) and from corporations. Further, although the actions of Super PACs were supposed to be independent of the campaigns they supported, candidates were allowed to participate directly in fundraising for the groups ("Working together . . . ," 2015). The result was that Republican candidates entered the 2014 campaign with well-stocked campaign war chests, and they were further supported by Super PACs that had even more money than the campaigns. Democrats, conversely, had less money for mounting their campaigns (Garrett, 2011).

In addition, a third issue had an impact in the 2010 elections—anti-Muslim attitudes. That anti-Muslim sentiment was largely absent from the 2006 midterms, despite the national unity that followed the 9/11 attacks. However, two factors appeared to make it an issue in 2010. The first was anti-Obama attitudes among Republicans, particularly those who argued that he was a Muslim. Second was the Republican attempt to make an issue out of plans to build a mosque near the Ground Zero Memorial in New York City (Tester, 2011). The contributions of those factors made anti-Islamic attitudes a consistent, if small, factor in the 2010 elections.

The result was a disaster for the Democratic Party. Their candidates were underfunded, in comparison to the opposition, and they received little assistance from outside groups. As a result, Democratic candidates lost a number of seats, particularly in the House of Representatives. Thus, the *New York Times* concluded that one lesson from the 2010 elections was that "more money can beat big money" (Lessing, 2011, A31).

There were counterarguments. LaRaja and Schaffner (2014) argued that the change in the law had little impact on elections. But Democrats disagreed. Further, long term, there was another major problem. The presence of the Tea Party in the 2010 election effectively destroyed the middle-of-the-road philosophy for both parties. Moderate candidates suddenly found it harder to win election, particularly within the Republican Party (Miller & Walling, 2011). Further, subsequent research has found that the law has changed the nature of local elections, with more local elections being influenced by national groups outside of the states in question (Hamm, et al., 2012).

CONCLUSIONS

Overall, Democrats lost a total of 63 seats in the 2010 elections (Simon & Palmer, 2011), with support for Democratic candidates declining sharply after March 2010 (Panagopolous, 2010). The extent to which those Democratic losses were caused by the financial disparity, and which were due to the Tea Party, can still be debated. However, the combination of those two factors were lethal to a number of Democratic campaigns—so bad that Rundle (2010) described the election as a "shellacking" for the Obama presidency. Bradley (2012) noted that it was an example of how voters can quickly change the political landscape of the nation. As Weatherford (2012) noted, the election became a negative referendum on President Barack Obama, despite his successful efforts to keep the nation from falling into an economic downturn. Campbell (2010) called the election a "triple wave election" because it was a criticism of Obama's economic plans and his health-care act, but also strengthened his chances for re-election in 2012.

Kolodny (2011) saw the election as the start of a period in which elections were going to be driven and influenced by volatile partisan differences. In that aspect, the 2010 elections were definitely a strong indication of partisanship. Even worse, that strong partisanship would continue over the next few years. In that sense, the culture of blame and payback was evident. Republicans viewed the 2010 election as a chance to even the score following their defeat by Obama in 2008. Further, 2010 marked the beginning of a series of Republican campaigns to stigmatize President Obama and others in the Democratic Party. That trend would reach its zenith in the House investigations of Hillary Clinton in the 2016 election, but that incident will be discussed more fully in a later chapter.

However, despite the bad news for Democrats in the House of Representatives, Republicans were unable to win control of the Senate. To some degree, Democrats held on to control of the Senate because they had some strong women candidates in some of those races, at a time when Republicans were taking hits for not being sensitive to women's issues; meanwhile, women candidates were generally viewed as more honest than their male opponents (Dolan, 2011).

There was, however, a new problem for the Republicans. While the Tea Party helped to engineer a takeover of the House, it also represented a new source of internal conflict for the GOP. Suddenly, being a conservative was not good enough. The Tea Party wanted far-right conservatives. That set up a future conflict between the moderates and the far right which only increased the dysfunction within Congress.

REFERENCES

Aldrich, J., Bishop, B., Hatch, R. Hillygus, D. S., & Rohde, D. (2014). Blame, responsibility, and the Tea Party in the 2010 midterm. *Political Behavior, 36,* 471–491.

Batum, J., Erikson, R. S., & Wiezien, C. (2010). *Forecasting House seats from generic congressional polls: The 2010 midterm election.* Paper presented at the annual meeting of the American Political Science Association.

Bond, J. R. (2013). 'Life ain't easy for a president named Barack': Party, ideology, and Tea Party freshman support for the nation's first black president. *Forum, 11,* 243–258.

Bradley, B. (2012, May 14). Citizens united. *Time, 179(19),* 23.

Brown, L. M. (2010, October). Restlessness unleashed: The Tea Partiers and the lessons of history. *Campaigns & Elections,* 36–41.

Bullock, C. S., & Hood, M. V. (2012). The Tea Party, Sarah Palin and the 2010 congressional elections: The aftermath of the election of Barack Obama. *Social Science Quarterly, 83,* 1424–1235.

Campbell, J. E. (2010). The midterm landslide of 2010: A triple wave election. *Forum, 8(4),* 1–19.

Carlson, M. (2012, August 9). Tea party brews trouble for Congress. *Birmingham News,* 7A.

Carson, J. L., & Pettigrew, S. (2013). Strategic politicians, partisan roll calls, and the Tea Party: Evaluating the 2010 midterm elections. *Electoral Studies, 32,* 26–36.

Chaves, E. K. (2011). *Money's been talking: How* Citizens United v. FEC *obfuscates the view of the role of wealth in our democracy.* Paper presented at the annual meeting of the American Political Science Association.

Citizens United at work: How the landmark decision legalized political coercion in the workplace. *Harvard Law Review, 128(2),* 669–690.

Cook, C. E. (2010). Preparing for the worst: Democrats' fears of the 2010 midterm elections. *Washington Quarterly, 33(2),* 183–189.

Courser, Z. (2010). The Tea Party at the election. *Forum, 8(4),* 1–18.

Dolan, K. (2011). *Evaluating women candidates: The impact of political gender stereotypes on voter choice in the 2010 midterm elections.* Paper presented at the annual meeting of the American Political Science Association.

Evers, K., Peterson, R., & Hadley, N. (2012). Principled or opportunist? Perceptions of Arlen Specter and his party switch during the 2010 midterm elections. *American Politics Research, 40,* 880–902.

Fang, L. (2014, November 10). How to buy an election. *Nation, 299(19),* 18–21.

Feldman, L. (2010, April 19). Tea Party eyes big prize: The 2010 midterm election. *Christian Science Monitor,* N.

Garrett, R. S. (2011). *The money fight: Themes in congressional campaign finance policy.* Paper presented at the annual meeting of the American Political Science Association.

Grunwald, M., & Crowley, M. (2010, November 15). Boiling Tea. *Time,* 36–37.

Hamm, K. E., Malbin, M. J., Kettler, J. J., & Gavin, B. (2012). *The impact of Citizens United in the States: Independent spending in state elections, 2006–2010.* Paper presented at the annual meeting of the American Political Science Association.

Jacobson, G. C. (2011). *The president, the Tea Party, and voting behavior in 2010: Insights from the Cooperative Congressional Election Study.* Paper presented at the annual meeting of the American Political Science Association.

Kitchens, J. T., & Powell, L. (2015). *The four pillars of politics: Why some candidates don't win and others can't lead.* Lanham, MD: Lexington.

Kolodny, R. (2011). The new normal: Partisan volatility and the U.S. midterm elections of 2010. *Representation, 47,* 231–239.

Kucera, J. (2010, June). The seeds of discontent. *U.S. News and World Report,* 40–41.

LaRaja, R., & Schaffner, B. J. (2014). The effects of campaign spending bans on electoral outcomes: Evidence from the states about the potential impact of *Citizens United v. FEC. Electoral Studies,* 102–114.

Lessing, L. (2011, November 17). More money can beat big money. *New York Times,* A31.

Mascaro, C. M., Novak, A. N., & Coggins, S. (2012). The daily brew: The structural evolution of the Coffee Party on Facebook during the 2010 United States midterm election season. *Journal of Information Technology & Politics, 9,* 234–253.

McDonald, M. (2010). Voter turnout in the 2010 midterm election. *Forum, 8(4),* 1–8.

Miller, W. J., & Walling, J. D. (2011). *Tea Party effects on 2010 U.S. elections: Stuck in the middle to lose.* Lanham, MD: Lexington.

Panagopolous, C. (2010). The dynamics of voter preference in the 2010 congressional midterm elections. *Forum, 8(4)*, 1–8.

Parker, C. S. (2013). *Change they can't believe in: The Tea Party and reactionary politics in America.* Princeton: Princeton University Press.

Raskin, J. (2012, October 8). Citizens United and the corporate court. *Nation, 295(15)*, 17–20.

Rundle, G. (2010). *The shellacking: The Obama presidency, the Tea Party, and the 2010 midterm elections.* London: K 1st Books.

Senior, J. (2010). The Benjamin Button election. *New York, 43(36)*, 28–108.

Simon, D. M., & Palmer, B. (2011). *The midterm elections of 2010: Another 'Year of the woman'?* Paper presented at the annual meeting of the Southern Political Science Association.

Skocpol, T., & Williamson, V. (2012). *The Tea Party and the remaking of American conservatism.* New York: Oxford University Press.

Smith, B. (2011, January 25). The incumbent's bane: Citizens United and the 2010 election. *Wall Street Journal*, A15.

Smith, M. M., & Powell, L. (2013). *Dark money, super PACs, and the 2012 election.* Lanham, MD: Lexington.

Stone, D. (2010, May 17). Tea Party 3.0 in Colorado. *Newsweek, 155(20)*, 6.

Stonecash, J. M. (2010). The 2010 elections: Party pursuits, voter perceptions, and the chancy game of politics. *Forum, 8(4)*, 1–12.

Tester, M. (2011). *President Obama and the influence of anti-Muslim sentiments in the 2010 midterm elections.* Paper presented at the annual meeting of the American Political Science Association.

Vacarri, C., & Nielsen, R. K. (2013). What drives politicians' online popularity? An analysis of the 2010 U.S. midterm elections. *Journal of Information Technology & Politics, 10(2)*, 208–222.

Weatherford, M. S. (2012). The wages of competence: Obama, the economy, and the 2010 midterm elections. *Presidential Studies Quarterly, 42*, 8–39.

Working together for an independent expenditure (2015). *Harvard Law Review, 128(5)*, 1478–1499.

ELEVEN

2012: Obama v. Romney

After four years of Barack Obama, Republicans were confident that they could defeat the incumbent president when he ran for re-election. Obama's job ratings were so low, they believed, he would lose to any Republican nominee. In retrospect, it seemed that they believed their own anti-Obama propaganda to such a degree that they assumed the voting public agreed with them. Their optimism turned out to be misplaced.

RICH MAN, POOR MAN

The Democrats turned out to be just as good at propaganda as the Republicans. During the summer of 2012, and before the fall campaign began, the Democrats were highly successful at painting Mitt Romney, the former governor and Republican nominee, as a rich man who was out of touch with middle America. Regardless, Romney continued to campaign on the basis of his business experience, adopting the typical Republican position that tax cuts for the rich were good for job creation. That position was discredited, however, when a nonpartisan study found no correlation between tax cuts for wealthy individuals and economic growth for the country as a whole (Weisman, 2002). Republicans were so upset with the report that they requested it be withdrawn, while the candidate kept talking up his business experience. As Balz (2012) wrote, "The best that can be said about how Mitt Romney fared in July is that he survived" (4A). As Blow (2012, Nov. 3) wrote, "The argument for electing Romney hinges on a sour economy and his experience as a businessman with the experience to turn it around" (A23). It simply didn't work. As Colorado political consultant Floyd Ciruli noted, Romney "felt the economy was going to be enough. It really wasn't" (quoted by Lightman & Wise, 2012, 21A).

Much of the Democratic success boiled down to money once again. After losing to Republican super PACs during the 2010 election, the Democrats quickly adopted the technique for themselves in 2012. They used much of that money in an independent campaign during the summer months to attack Romney for his past business practices, particularly instances in which his Bain Capital purchased factories, shut them down, and moved their jobs overseas (Confessore & McGinty, 2012; Milbank, 2012).

For the most part, though, Republican strategists attempted to avoid using economic issues as part of the campaign. As Kristof (2012) wrote, "Republican leaders in 2012 have a natural winning issue—the limping economy—but they seem determined to scare away centrist voters with extreme positions on everything from abortion to sex education" (SR 11). Similarly, Douthat (2012) described Romney's campaign style as "studied vagueness and generic Republican rhetoric" (SR9).

Collins (2012) characterized the Republican position on wealth as "Only the good get rich" (A19). Similarly, Krugman (2012, Oct. 12) wrote, "Republicans . . . are committed to an economic doctrine that has proved false, indeed disastrous, in other countries" (A23). Dowd (2012) noted that there was an image of unreality tied to the Republican candidate; thus she wrote, "It was remarkable to watch Mitt Romney . . . reach deep inside himself to give a speech in which he appeared genuine. It was also remarkable to see that even when he looks genuine, he still seems fake" (SR1). Overall, Romney seemed to have trouble handling his wealth while trying to relate to average voters. As Carlson (2012) wrote, "Romney's personal fortune has proved to be a tender subject as well as the source material for many of his worst gaffes" (7A).

Romney was hurt further by the Obama campaign's financial advantage, even after the conventions. The Democrats raised $181 million in the month of September alone (Confessore, 2012). In the first few weeks after the conventions, the pro-Obama forces aired more than 92,000 television ads, 32 percent more than Romney. In fact, the Obama campaign had an advantage over Romney in 14 of the top 15 media markets (Moore & Schouten, 2012). As a result, the Republicans in Congress were starting to feel the pain of their constant fight against Democrats. A plurality of 44 percent of American voters blamed the gridlock in Washington on the GOP, while only 29 percent thought the Democrats were at fault (Steinhauer & Weisman, 2012). The problem became so acute for Republican congressmen that Steinhauer and Weisman stated, "Some House races may turn on shaking the Tea Party label" (A17). Friedman (2012) noted that Romney essentially quit trying to bother to even target Tea Party voters in the general election. In the end, no improvement on that front came out of the election (Krugman, 2016, Nov. 2). Meanwhile, in the final month of the campaign, Obama targeted Romney for having outdated ideas on the issue (Page, 2012, Oct. 22). Similarly, Bruni (2012, Oct. 28) wrote, "Obama's greatest gift has been Romney himself, whose wealth, his tin-eared allusions to it, his offshore accounts and his unreleased tax returns, are an especially awkward fit for a moment of increased anxiety about income inequality" (SR3).

Obama won, the Republicans retained control of the House, and the gridlock in Congress continued. The final blow in this campaign turned out to be self-inflicted by Romney himself. In a private fund-raising event, Romney was captured on tape saying that 47 percent of the voters would never vote for him, because that many were dependent on the federal government for handouts (Landler, 2012; Moore, 2012). Columnist Eugene Robinson (2012) described the Romney statement as that of "diligent 'us' vs. lazy 'them'" (7A). Obama's only mistake on the issue was that he never brought the statement up during his first debate (Tucker, 2012). After the release of the tape, polling indicated that Obama had a lead nationally and in key electoral states, giving Romney little chance of winning (Zeleny & Rutenberg, 2012, Sept. 21).

THE IRRELEVANCE OF DEBATES

Forget about the supposed importance of the 1960 debates in propelling John Kennedy to victory. That might have been true then, but not in 2012, when 70 million voters tuned in for the first debate in early October (Stetler, 2012). Barack Obama opened the three debate series with a truly awful performance, particularly for someone who was known for being so adept at speechmaking. In fact, his first debate was amazingly lackluster, with the President displaying little enthusiasm for the event. He almost seemed to dismiss it as something not worthy of his attention. Romney, by contrast, was energized and equipped with enough information to impress viewers with his preparation. Not surprisingly, Romney exhibited a stark increase in morale following his performance, while the Obama campaign was hit with "a new sense of urgency" following his weak performance (Rutenberg & Baker, 2012, A12).

Romney's only mistake was a criticism of PBS that was viewed by some as an attack on the "Big Bird" character from the *Sesame Street* show (Blow, 2012, Oct. 6). As Cass (2012) wrote, "Mitt Romney . . . shows an easy confidence that suits a presidential contender. Barack Obama sounds like a long-winded professor a tad annoyed at having to go over this stuff one more time for the students in the back." And, Cass continued, "Romney demonstrated that he can boil down his points in simple, pragmatic language," while "Obama . . . sometimes seemed momentarily lost as he lapsed into this trademark pauses during long answers." (19A).

Not surprisingly, both candidates soon embarked on a "They started it" exchange of negative attacks, with each denouncing the other for unfair attacks. As Shear (2012, Aug. 10) wrote, it was "An election season where the whining is almost as loud as the barrage of ads" (A10). Ruten-berg (2012, Aug. 17) agreed, writing that "It's a slugfest on the campaign trail," and adding that the Republican convention has not elevated the tone of the presidential campaign" (A15). Similarly, Bruni (2016, Aug. 5) wrote, it is ". . . a presidential campaign in which each candidate's main pitch—*I'm not half as awful as the other guy*—points everything in a nega-tive direction" (SR3).

The contrasting views of the two candidates were obvious by the sec-ond week in September. By then, the Obama campaign thought the elec-tion was essentially over and all they had to do was to hold onto the lead they had developed during the summer; Romney, by contrast, argued that all of Obama's early spending was a waste of money (Zeleny, 2012). Thus, as Berg (2012) wrote, there were relatively few undecided voters available to respond to both campaigns' persuasive efforts, and many of those lived in states such as New York or California where the electoral delegates were never in doubt. Further, the Romney team and the Repub-lican National Committee combined to raise $100 million during August, enough for the Republicans to buy air time in support of their candidate (Gillum & Beaumont, 2012). Together, the two campaigns combined to raise a record $2 billion for the election (Schouten & Schmaars, 2012; Confessore & Willis, 2012).

Unfortunately for Romney, he was wrong. In fact, the election may have been over even earlier than the summer. Polling data found that, prior to the first partisan primary, only six percent of the voters were undecided (Vavreck, 2012). Further, the political conventions had little impact on voting intention (Nagourney, 2012), although Obama did re-ceive a slight bounce from his (Page, 2012, Sept. 10). And Obama main-tained his lead over Romney despite his poor debate performance (Silver, 2012). Apparently, voters decided whether they were for or against Ba-rack Obama early in the electoral process.

RACISM, AGAIN

After four years of attacks from Republicans in Congress, Barack Obama was highly unpopular with many Republican voters. Part of their dis-satisfaction with him was his health care program, which had passed Congress but was hated by many Republican lawmakers. However, part of the hatred appeared to be related to continued racism, possibly as a holdover from the 2008 election. There were still those who didn't believe he was an American citizen, and others who believed he was a closet Muslim. In fact, one lawsuit was filed in Kansas in an effort to keep Obama off the ballot, arguing that he had not been born in the United States, but it was thrown out of court in September long before the elec-tion (Eligon, 2012).

Such ideas seemed to be particularly prevalent among white, blue-collar voters. Research later reported that many attitudes toward Obama were directly influenced by anti-black sentiment (Pasek, et al, 2014). As *The New York Times* reported, "Part of the explanation is in the socially conservative views that many of these voters have on issues such as abortion, gay marriage, and gun control. And a small, but hard-to-measure, part in this election is lingering racism attitudes toward the first black president" ("Why the Democrats trail . . . , 2012, 10A). When the voting was completed, the 2012 election went down as one of the most racially polarizing campaigns ever (Powers, 2014).

MICROTARGETING, AGAIN

If Barack Obama seemed to dismiss the debates as unimportant, maybe that's because he didn't really expect them to have much impact. His major campaign strategy, it turned out, was to revert to the micro-targeting that worked so well for him in 2008. For the 2012 election, the campaign made one major adjustment. As they prepared, the Obama campaign made a simple but effective assumption. If the team could get every Obama voter from 2008 to vote for him again, then they would win—regardless of how successful the Romney campaign might be.

To support this approach, the Obama team again used microtargeting supported by phone banks in an effort to contact voters who had supported him in 2008. As part of that effort, they were able to identify approximately one million supporters from that election who were undecided or leaning away from Obama for 2012. Those one million voters became the main target of Obama's turnout efforts. The microtargeting approach identified many of them in terms of home address and media behavior. The data were then used to target individuals on the Internet with specific digital ads for their demographic (Singer & Duhigg, 2012).

Both sides believed that voter turnout could be the deciding factor (Weinschenk, 2015), particularly in the delegate-rich state of Ohio (Davey & Wines, 2012). In fact, both also seemed haunted by the closeness of the 2000 election, with both teams organizing legal teams that involved thousands of lawyers who were ready to go into close elections that might be contested by either side (Bronner, 2012; Korte, 2012).

Obama, of course, won, perhaps because his approach was so much more sophisticated than that of the Republicans. His campaign made extensive use of data and employed subtle techniques to try to influence habits on election day. Their overall approach was similar to marketing efforts of credit card companies and big-box retailers. Targeted voters were personally contacted by callers who had detailed information about their lives. Those voters were then asked detailed questions, such as "What time will you vote?" and "What route will you use to drive to the polls?" The Obama's team research indicated that simply asking such questions was likely to increase turnout (Duhigg, 2012).

Obama also had a more extensive organization than did Romney. Even worse for the Romney campaign, one of its organizers in Virginia was arrested for fraud (Saul, 2012). In addition, the Obama campaign made a major effort to get its voters to the polls early; as part of this effort, Obama set an example by voting early himself, becoming the first president to ever do so (Barbaro & Baker, 2012). Both sides listed Latinos as their main target in three key states—Colorado, Florida, and Nevada—but the Obama campaign had a two-to-one advantage in those states over Romney (Nagourney & Santos, 2012). In some instances, both campaigns were successful at increasing turnout. In Ohio, which was eventually won by Obama, early data indicated that overall turnout would be up, buoyed by the turnout efforts of both campaigns (Stephens-Davidowitz, 2012). Zeleny and Rutenberg (2012, Oct. 28) noted that in the swing states, the final days of campaigning were occurring on a county-by-county basis. Much of that work was what Rutenberg (2012, Oct. 26) described as "grunt work" (A1). With two weeks remaining, Romney had a two-point lead in Florida (Madhani, 2012), but the Obama canvassing effort made up the difference and won there. In two other key states, Iowa and Wisconsin, Obama entered the final weeks with a six-point lead in the former and an eight-point lead in the latter (Shear, 2012, Oct. 19).

In the final days, it became a matter of moves and countermoves. When it looked like Obama was getting ahead in Virginia, Romney tried to offset that edge by targeting coal miners in the western part of the state (Shear, 2012, Oct. 27). Obama responded by focusing more on women voters in the state (Huetteman & Shear, (2012). That strategy paid off, as Obama ended up winning the state. Romney also tried to overtake Obama in Colorado with a strong turnout program (Healy, 2012), but that effort also came up short.

Still, Lightman (2012) noted that it wasn't easy, partly because Romney supplemented his targeting efforts by using evangelicals to mobilize voters (Kucinich, 2012). In the end, Lightman noted, Obama "held onto the coalition that led him to victory in 2008: Latinos, African-Americans and young people" (19A). The problem, though, was the divisive nature of that win. As McCormick and Giroux (2012) wrote after analyzing exit polls from the election, "The American electorate divided like two foreign lands, split between men and women, whites and minorities, rich and poor and young and old," with Obama winning minority and young voters, while Romney won whites and those over the age of 65 (20A). Obama's support was particularly high among Latino voters (Wallace, 2012), aided by Republican opposition to immigration reform (Barelto & Collingwood, 2015).

CONCLUSIONS

Much of the 2012 campaign revolved around the political pillar of consumerism. The Romney campaign team based its messages on the perception that Obama had been in charge of a weak economy. That assumption did not hold. In August, hiring increased as more jobs were created (Rampell, 2012). The economy continued to make steady, if unspectacular gains, buoyed in part by solid growth in the housing industry (Schmit, 2012).

A secondary series of messages revolved around narcissism or, as the *New York Times* called it, "American exceptionalism" (Shane, 2012). As Scott wrote, "Is America the greatest country? Candidates had better say so." But, he added, this issue was largely one of distraction from the bigger issue of the economy. Thus he wrote, "Of course, the reason talking directly about serious American problems is risky is that most voters don't like it" (SR6).

At the same time, Obama demonstrated that a candidate could win a presidential election without being exceptional in the debates. Further, he won despite a series of racist arguments that the opposition thought would undermine his campaign. In that sense, members of the voting public illustrated that their approach to presidential politics rose above that of some candidates.

The ultimate factor deciding the election was likely that of microtargeting. From that perspective, the Democrats were finally learning how to do it well. For years, the Democratic Party had attempted a variety of GOTV (Get Out The Votes) efforts (Kitchens & Powell, 2015), but those efforts became highly sophisticated in 2012. They had learned how to encourage their supporters to vote.

More and more though, both parties were beginning to spend more time, energy, and money into "gaming" elections. The toy was beginning to be the American people, but perhaps the voting public was getting tired of being played.

REFERENCES

Balz, D. (2012, August 5). August a pivotal month for Romney. *Birmingham News*, 4A.

Barbaro, M., & Baker, (2012, October 26). On a frenetic day, Obama votes and Romney is for change. *New York Times*, A20.

Barelto, M. A., & Collingwood, L. (2015). Group-based appeals and the Latino vote in 2012: How immigration became a mobilizing issue. *Electoral Studies, 40*, 490–499.

Berg, R. (2012, August 17). Few voters are truly up for grabs, research shows. *New York Times*, A14.

Blow, C. M. (2012, October 6). Don't mess with Big Bird. *New York Times*, A17.

Blow, C. M. (2012, November 3). Is Romney unraveling? *New York Times*, A23.

Bronner, E. (2012, November 2). Campaigns brace to sue for votes in crucial states. *New York Times*, A1, A14.

Bruni, F. (2012, August 5). Truculence before truth. *New York Times*, SR3.

Bruni, F. (2012, October 28). Obama's squandered advantages. *New York Times,* SR3.

Carlson, M. (2012, August 6). Romney has problem with being wealthy. *Birmingham News,* 7A.

Cass, C. (2012, October 7). What we learned from the debate. *Birmingham News,* 19A.

Collins, G. (2012, September 1). Only the good get rich. *New York Times,* A19.

Confessore, N. (2012, October 7). Record haul for Democrats in September. *New York Times,* A17.

Confessore, N., & McGinty, J. C. (2012, August 5). Record spending by Obama's camp shrivels coffers. *New York Times,* A1, A14.

Confessore, N., & Willis, D. (2012, October 26). Presidential candidates are on track for $2 billion. *New York Times,* A16, A18.

Davey, M., & Wines, M. (2012, November 4). In Ohio, a study in contrasts as 2 campaigns get out vote. *New York Times,* A1, A20.

Douthat, R. (2012, September 2). Franklin Delano Romney. *New York Times,* SR9.

Dowd, M. (2012, September 2). Cruel conservatives throw a masquerade ball. *New York Times,* SR1, SR11.

Duhigg, C. (2012, October 14). Campaigns mine personal lives to get out vote. *New York Times,* A1, A14.

Eligon, J. (2012, September 15). Ballot challenge in Kansas over Obama's birth is ended. *New York Times,* A12.

Friedman, T. L. (2012, November 4). The morning after the morning after. *New York Times,* SR13.

Gillum, J., & Beaumont, T. (2012, September 5). RNC, Romney campaign raise $100M in August. *Birmingham News,* 3A.

Healy, J. (2012, August 5). Romney campaign takes to the ground in Colorado. *New York Times,* A14.

Huetteman, E., & Shear, M. D. (2012, October 20). Campaigning in Virginia, Obama presses for women's vote. *New York Times,* 15A.

Kitchens, J. T., & Powell, L. (2015). *The four pillars of politics: Why some candidates don't win and others can't lead.* Lanham, MD: Lexington.

Korte, G. (2012, October 30). Both sides arming for voter recounts. *USA Today,* 2A.

Kristof, N. D. (2012, September 2). Scaring the voters in the middle. *New York Times,* SR11.

Krugman, (2012, October 12). Triumph of the wrong? *New York Times,* A23.

Krugman, (2012, November 2). The blackmail caucus. *New York Times,* A25.

Kucinich, J. (2012, October 18). Evangelicals mobilize for Romney/Ryan campaign. *USA Today,* 4A.

Landler, M. (2012, September 21). Obama seizes on Romney comments, suggesting he is out of touch. *New York Times,* A12.

Lightman, D. (2012, November 7). Obama wins re-election after bruising campaign. *Birmingham News,* 19A.

Lightman, D,, & Wise, L. (2012, November 7). Romney couldn't translate vision. *Birmingham News,* 21A.

Madhani, A. (2012, October 22). Battle for Florida heats up. *USA Today,* 4A.

McCormick, J., & Giroux, G. (2012, November 7). Exit polls show sharp divisions in electorate. *Birmingham News,* 20A.

Milbank, D, (2012, August 9). Mitt Romney's capitalist game. *Birmingham News,* 7A.

Moore, M. T. (2012, September 19). Romney's comments unnoticed for months. *USA Today,* 6A.

Moore, M. T., & Schouten, F. (2012, October 4). Dems' ad blitz puts GOP on spot. *USA Today,* 4A.

Nagourney, A. (2012, September 8). Conventions draw crowds but sway few voters. *New York Times,* A8-A9.

Nagourney, A., & Santos, F. (2012, October 19). Both parties see Latino voters as the deciders in 3 key states. *New York Times,* A1, A17.

Page, S. (2012, September 10). Obama gets a slight bounce from convention. *USA Today*, 4A.

Page,- S. (2012, October 22). Obama casts Romney as outdated. *USA Today*, 4A.

Pasek, J., Stark, T. H., Krosnick, J. A., Tompson, T., & Payne, B. K. (2014). Attitudes toward Blacks in the Obama era. *Public Opinion Quarterly, 78(S1)*, 276–302.

Powers, J. M. (2014). Statistical evidence of racially polarized voting in the Obama elections, and implications for Section 2 of the Voting Rights Act. *Georgetown Law Journal, 102*, 881–925.

Rampell, C. (2012, August 4). Hiring picks up, but data gives no clear signal. *New York Times*, A1, B6.

Robinson, E. (2012, September 22). Romney's class warfare: Diligent 'us' vs. lazy 'them.' *Birmingham News*, 7A.

Rutenberg, J. (2012, August 17). The lowest common denominator and the 2012 race for president. *New York Times*, A15.

Rutenberg, J. (2012, October 26). To Obama workers, winning takes grunt work and math. *New York Times*, A1, A19.

Rutenberg, J., & P. Baker, (2012, October 5). Campaign gains a new intensity in debate's wake. *New York Times*, A1, A12.

Saul, S. (2012, October 20). Man aiding G.O.P. effort in vote drive is charged. *New York Times*, A15.

Schmit, J. (2012, October 18). Housing surge looks solid. *USA Today*, 1A.

Schouten, F. (2012, October 18). A fierce ground war for votes. *USA Today*, 1A-2A.

Schouten, F., & Schmaars, C. (2012, October 22). GOP has edge in overall cash on hand. *USA Today*, 1A.

Shane, S. (2012, October 21). The opiate of exceptionalism. *New York Times*, SR6.

Shear, M. D. (2012, August 10). The 2012 cycle: Attack, feign outrage, repeat. *New York Times*, A10.

Shear, M. D. (2012, October 19). Two battlegrounds: Polls show leads for Obama. *New York Times*, A18.

Shear, M. D. (2012, October 27). In Virginia, Romney scours coal country for edge over Obama. *New York Times*, A1, A10.

Silver, N. (2012, October 12). A bounce for Romney, but just how high? *New York Times*, A11.

Singer, N., & Duhigg, C. (2012, October 28). Tracking clicks online to try to sway voters. *New York Times*, A12-A13.

Steinhauer, J., & Weisman, J. (2012, September 16). Some Republicans try out a new campaign theme: bipartisanship. *New York Times*, A16–A17.

Stetler, B. (2012, October 5). Presidential debate draws over 70 million viewers. *New York Times*, A12.

Stephens-Davidowitz, S. (2012, October 21). Google's crystal ball. *New York Times*, SR1, SR6.

Tucker, C. (2012, October 10). Obama's defeat. *Birmingham News*, 10A.

Vavreck, L. (2012, September 23). Hark! The undecideds! *New York Times*, SR3.

Wallace, S. J. (2012). It's complicated: Latinos, President Obama and the 2012 election. *Social Science Quarterly, 93*, 1360–1383.

Weinschenk, A. C. (2015). Polls and elections: Campaign field offices and voter mobilization in 2012. *Presidential Studies Quarterly, 45*, 573–580.

Weisman, J. (2012, November 2). Tax report withdrawn at request of G.O.P. *New York Times*, B1, B5.

Why the Democrats trail among white, blue-collar voters (2012, September 6). *USA Today*, 10A.

Zeleny, J. (2012, September 9). Just 58 days from the election, a guide on 5 factors to watch. *New York Times*, A1, A16.

Zeleny, J., & Rutenberg, J. (2012, September 21). Romney faces an uphill fight to win at polls. *New York Times*, A1, A13.

TWELVE

2014: Republicans Take the Senate

Following the 2012 election, the Republican Party in Washington faced two disappointments. Barack Obama had won re-election as president. Even worse, the Democrats had maintained control of the U.S. Senate. There was nothing the GOP could do immediately about the presidency, but the Senate was another matter. Thus the Republicans turned their attention to taking control of the Senate away from the Democrats. Meanwhile, in the House, Republicans were still trying to deal with their rebellious Tea Party members.

THE TEA PARTY

John Boehner and other Republican leaders in the Senate wanted to do something to make their party more appealing to Latinos. In fact, advocates for a change in immigration law had targeted Republicans for that purpose (Parker, 2013). Their plan called for legislation that would allow some undocumented immigrants to gain legal status. However, those advocates totally underestimated the reaction from within their own ranks. Instead of party support, the GOP found itself facing opposition from within its own party, particularly from the Tea Party. The Tea Party bombarded Republican members of Congress with angry phone calls and e-mails, many coming under the hashtag of "#NoAmnesty" (Weisman & Parker, 2014). Meanwhile, the Republicans were further hindered by views of some of their members that the poor, including immigrants, were "morally inferior" (Egan, 2013). The only question was whether the president himself would be a target for campaign messages, or whether the focus would be on his issues instead (Peters, 2013).

In large measure both the Democrats and the moderate Republicans were trying to prevent the Tea Party from achieving significant success.

That meant that Republicans had advantages in seven key states. In one, however, the Democrats saw an edge—Kansas. The Republican from Kansas was 76-year-old Pat Roberts, a candidate at odds with the Tea Party in the state (Martin, 2014b). Roberts was further hindered by the fact that he didn't own or rent a house in the state. The combination of problems gave Democrats hope in the state, with Roberts becoming an "emblem of Washington status" (A1). Generally, the Tea Party found itself disappointed with a number of moderate Republicans, but were generally ineffective at mounting opposition to those candidates in the primaries (Martin, 2014c). As Martin noted, "The Tea Party may be nudging Republicans to the right in Congress with the implicit threat of primary challenges, but when it comes to recruiting quality challengers, it is falling decidedly short" (A1). The Tea Party even recruited a candidate to run against Republican Senate leader Mitch McConnell in Kentucky, to little avail (Weisman, 2014b). Consequently, mainline Republicans saw an opportunity to take control in many campaigns (Martin, 2014e).

However, the Tea Party had one major win, a surprise upset of Republican House leader Eric Cantor in Virginia—an election that was followed by a sudden drop in stock prices on Wall Street (Peters & Dewan, 2014). As Martin (2014f) wrote, "Mr. Cantor's defeat, the most unexpected of a congressional leader in recent memory will reverberate in the capital and could have major implications for an immigration overhaul" (A1). Despite the rarity of the upset, Weisman (2014c) predicted that the election would have a subdued effect on the other Republicans in the House. As Dionne (2014) wrote, "The Republican leaders happily rode the Tea Party tiger while doing so was convenient. Now, Cantor has fallen to the very forces he and his colleagues unleashed and encouraged. . . . [Now] they are likely to cower and accommodate even more" (43).

The only Republican senator to face serious Tea Party opposition was Thad Cochran in Mississippi, and he won re-election with the help of moderate Democrats (Parker & Martin, 2014). Cochran's Republican opponent presented a moderate image in public, but was a hard-right candidate on Mississippi radio. On the radio dials, the opponent, Chris McDaniel, said he would move to Mexico rather than pay reparations over slavery, and called Mexican women "mamacitas" (Weisman, 2014b, A17). Super PACs countered by spending money to help Cochran (Martin, 2014a).

Tea Party Republicans also tried to take advantage of the common core issue related to education (Martin, 2014d). The theory was that most voters were upset with the program, originated by other Republicans, of a common group of required learning objectives for all public schools. The new standards faced opposition from both conservatives and liberals. As *New York Times* columnist David Brooks (2014) wrote, "the Common Core education standards, which are being attacked on the right because they are common and on the left because they are core" (A21).

THE SENATE

The Democrats knew the Republicans would make a major push to control the Senate in 2014. That's why the Democrats started early in 2013 in an effort to block the GOP effort (Confessore, 2013). But disappointment soon became apparent. The party, for example, was hoping that actress Ashley Judd would challenge Mitch McConnell in the Kentucky senate campaign, but she declined to do so (Camia, 2013), thus hurting the party's chances. Meanwhile, the GOP enhanced the ability of their incumbents gaining re-election by announcing they would punish any party consultants who worked in primaries against those incumbents (2013).

In individual contests, Democratic Senate candidates sometimes distanced themselves from an unpopular President Obama (Martin & Parker, 2014). Thus they wrote, "Democrats are becoming increasingly alarmed about their midterm election fortunes amid President Obama's sinking approval ratings, a loss in a special election in Florida last week, and millions of dollars spent by Republican-aligned groups attacking the new health law" (A1). That included West Virginia, where Secretary of State Natalie Tennant avoided mentioning Obama, even though Michelle Obama had headlined a fund-raiser for her (Gabriel, 2013). Democrats often complained that they received little aid from Obama because "his vaulted political organization has done little to help the party's vulnerable congressional candidates" (Martin & Parker, 2014, A1).

Republicans also tried to cut into the Democratic advantage in technology by recruiting their own workers from Silicon Valley (Richtel & Confessore, 2014). Their efforts achieved minimum success, simply because so many of the workers in the industry leaned toward the Democrats.

Meanwhile, Republican consultant Karl Rove (2014) predicted that the races were going to get dirty as both parties sought an electoral advantage. Republicans started with leads in three states lost by Obama in 2012—West Virginia, South Dakota, and Montana. There were four additional red states where Senate Democrats were trying to hold on—Alaska, Arkansas, Louisiana, and North Carolina. As Rove wrote, "An incumbent with much higher name recognition than an opponent, but only a narrow lead this early on, is evidence of a low ceiling of support. It also suggests that the challenger can rise as his background, values and agenda become better known" (A15). That perception of vulnerability was particularly pronounced in North Carolina, where seven Republican opponents fought it out in the primary for the chance to face Democrat Kay Hagan in the general election (Parker, 2014b).

However, Rove's Crossroads Group seemed to lose power in the 2014 cycle (Confessore, 2014a). Despite Rove's prediction of negative campaigns, the early Super PAC ads for Republicans were positive in tone. Parker (2014c) attributed the positive approach to lessons learned from the 2012 campaign "when Mitt Romney and outside Republican groups largely failed to offer an alternate message to an onslaught of negative spots, and the increasing prevalence of stock footage made public by campaigns that makes producing positive ads easier" (A14). The results became a self-fulfilling prophecy, as an increasing number of voters expected the Republicans to win control of both the Senate and the House (Dewberry, 2014).

Democrats also faced a financial disadvantage, with outside groups stepping in to help the Republicans (c, 2014b). A court ruling, resulting from a lawsuit filed by Alabama businessman Shaun McCutcheon (Nielson, 2014; Bravin, 2014), led to a decision that increased the amount of money that could be given to federal candidates. Chief Justice John Roberts justified the decision, noting that "Money in politics may at times seem repugnant to some, but so does much of what the First Amendment vigorously protects" (quoted by Wolf & Schouten, 2014, 1A). The decision led both parties to intensify their fund-raising efforts (Confessore, 2014b). Some Republicans even tried to expand their fund-raising lists by offering a gun sweepstakes, with the winner getting a new rifle or shotgun (Peters, 2014).

Even without the McCutcheon decision, the Republicans had a lot of money. The Koch brothers alone, who spent freely on independent expenditures in the 2012 election, vowed to spend $30 million to help Republicans regain control of the Senate (Peters & Hulse, 2014). The Democrats responded by drawing attention to some subsidiaries of the brothers: "a chemical plant in North Carolina, an oil refinery in Alaska, a lumber operation in Arkansas . . ." [and a focus on the companies] "that cut jobs and prized the bottom line over the well-being of its employees" (A1).

There were some other Democratic successes. In New Jersey, Cory Booker defeated a Tea Party opponent named Steve Lonegan, giving Democrats 55 seats in 2013 (Moore, 2013). Still, the 2014 election cycle looked like it could be a problem for Democrats, partly because disenchantment with Obama's health law was growing (Weisman, 2013b). The bigger positive news for Democrats was that their fund-raising was going well, bolstered by new money coming to the party from women donors (Steinhauer, 2013).

Still, many Democratic candidates felt like they were vulnerable to a challenge (Krauthammer, 2013; Weisman, 2013c) and even shook the Obama presidency (Page, 2013). Despite those concerns, the Obama healthcare plan seemed to have become an accepted part of government policy. As Douthat (2013b) wrote, "It's still likely that Obamacare will be undone only if its critics are willing to do something more painful, and take their own turn wrestling with a system that resists any kind of change" (SR13). Blow (2013c) put it differently, writing that "Change is hard and often messy, and Obamacare is change" (A23). Similarly, Krugman (2014b) wrote, "When it comes to health reform, Republicans suffer from delusions of disaster. They know, just know, that the Affordable Care Act is doomed to utter failure, so failure is what they have seen, never mind the facts on the ground" (A21). Eventually, the Democrats got a key win when the Supreme Court, with help by a vote from Chief Justice John Roberts, upheld the health-care law despite a legal challenge from Republicans (Douthat, 2013a). A second boost came later when more than eight million people signed up for the insurance program (Landler & Shear, 2014). As a result, as the campaign progressed, an increasing number of Democrats were vocal in their support of the healthcare law (Parker, 2014d).

There was some good news for the Democrats, particularly in terms of the immigration issue. President Obama sent a proposal to Congress that would offer a path to citizenship for some individuals who were in the nation illegally. As Blow (2013b) wrote, Obama's proposal was "a brilliant turn to immigration reform. Either he gets it, which would be a blow to Republican electoral hopes, or Republicans fight it (which would turn off Hispanics for years)." And, he added, "They [Republicans] have been blinded by that anger. The president knows that. And he knows that blind soldiers don't often win battles. In choosing to pivot to immigration reform, he has created a win-win scenario for himself and the Democrats. Clever, clever" (A17). In the end, though, his proposal gained little traction and he staggered into the 2014 election with a host of negative ratings (Clark & Kumar, 2013). As Clark and Kumar concluded, "A majority of voters don't trust him or don't have confidence in his leadership" (17A).

Democrats got another boost in December 2013 when President Obama gave a major speech on income inequality in the nation (Krugman, 2013). As Krugman wrote, "Obama laid out a disturbing—and, unfortunately, all too accurate—vision of an America losing touch with its own ideals, an erstwhile land of opportunity becoming a class-ridden society" (A31). It established income inequality as an issue that Democrats hoped would be to their benefit in the 2014 election. Along this line, Democrats also got a boost when Republican efforts to restrict access by black voters to elections also got struck down by the courts (Douthat, 2013b).

Democrats also tried to take advantage of their enhanced voter turnout program. They spent a great deal of time and effort on voter registration and turnout programs in ten states, spending $60 million and sending 4,000 paid staff members to the states (Parker, 2014a). Their targets were African-Americans, Hispanics, unmarried women, and younger voters. Their goal was to limit the turnout drops in non-presidential elections in which one-third of Democratic voters did not show up to vote.

There was hope among Democrats that the improved economy might help their chances. After all, President Obama had inherited a damaged economy, and his programs had largely been successful in leading the nation out of the economic quagmire. By mid-year, job growth was making remarkable gains (Schwartz, 2014). But wages remained flat for many Americans, and Obama's job ratings remained low. That situation caused Shear (2014) to write that "the positive economic news is no guarantee of electoral success for the Democrats, even if the trend continues through the summer" (A12). Similarly, Krugman (2014b) wrote, "there's an even stronger case to be made that high unemployment, by destroying workers' bargaining power has become a major source of rising inequality and stagnating incomes even for those lucky enough to have jobs" (A25). The final result of the economic situation is that Democrats had little to gain from it.

Meanwhile, Republicans faced their own problems. Specifically, the party had been unable to develop any reasonable plan for attracting minority voters (West, 2013; Blow, 2013a). As Blow wrote, "Too many House Republican districts are isolated in naturally homogeneous areas or gerrymandered ghettos, so elected officials there rarely hear or see the great and growing diversity of this country and the infusion of energy and ideas and art with which it enriches us" (A19). The situation perhaps imposed some false hopes for Democrats, who felt that the Republicans had overplayed their hand by "crying wolf" for the previous four years. As Powers (2013) wrote, "We are coming off four years of being oversold on one fantastical story after another on the evils of Obamaland that didn't pan out" (7A). Republicans were still highly optimistic, debating only how far they should take targets for the 2014 campaigns (Weisman, 2013a).

CONCLUSIONS

When the dust settled on the 2014 elections, the Republicans had gained enough seats in the Senate to take control of the body. That meant they controlled both legislative bodies, even though Democrats retained control of the presidency. That meant that the mechanism for gridlock remained, with both parties in a position to blame each other for governmental inaction.

Meanwhile, as the 2014 elections commenced, there were increased calls for Congress to return to the art of compromise, but the Tea Party resisted those efforts. As Friedman (2014) wrote, for the Tea Party, "calling someone a 'deal maker' is now the ultimate put-down" (SR11). The opposing view was expressed by former senator Alan Simpson, who said, "if you can't learn to compromise yourself, you should not be in Congress, be in business, or get married" (quoted by Friedman, 2014, SR11). As the impasse in Congress continued to harden, members found it increasingly difficult to get anything done, even on local bills that had bipartisan support. The fear of compromise made it difficult to even pass those relatively minor bits of legislation (Hulse, 2014). In the end, no progress was made. Congress ended the year just as deadlocked as it began, with the only change coming when Republicans won enough Senate seats to take control of that legislative body too.

The remarkable thing about the 2014 election, however, was it had little impact on governmental dysfunction. Both parties were still engaged in parent-child behavior, blaming each other for the problem. Republican control of Congress was countered by Democratic control of the presidency. And, even within Congress, right-wing Republicans were still at odds with the party's moderates. Nothing, it seemed, was going to get done.

REFERENCES

Blow, C. M. (2013a, March 30). The G.O.P.'s diversity deserts. *New York Times,* A19.

Blow, C. M. (2013b, October 19). The president's pivot. *New York Times,* A17.

Blow, C. M. (2013c, November 23). Trouble don't last always. *New York Times,* A23.

Bravin, J. (2014, April 3). High Court ends limit on donations. *Wall Street Journal,* A1, A4.

Brooks, D. (2014, April 18). When the circus descends. *New York Times,* A21.

Camia, C. (2013, March 28). Judd says next role won't be as senator. *USA Today,* 3A.

Clark, L., & Kumar, A. (2013, December 29). A year of setbacks. *Birmingham News,* 17A.

Confessore, N. (2013, November 15). Groups mobilize to aid Democrats in '14 data arms race. *New York Times,* A17.

Confessore, N. (2014a, February 2). Rebel conservatives excel in G.O.P. fund-raising, heralding a tug right. *New York Times,* A19.

Confessore, N. (2014b, April 5). Ruling spurs rush for cash in both parties. *New York Times,* A1, A15.

Confessore, N. (2014c, April 12). Big G.O.P. donors stir Senate runs. *New York Times,* A1, A13.

Dewberry, David R. (2014). *The third-person effect goes to Congress.* Paper presented at the annual meeting of the Southern States Communication Association, New Orleans.

Dionne, E. J. (2014, June 15). Eric Cantor and the tea party purge. *Birmingham News,* 43.

Douthat, R. (2013a, June 30). Democrats get a gift from the Roberts court. *New York Times,* SR11.

Douthat, R. (2013b, November 17). The three burials of Obamacare. *New York Times,* SR13.

Egan, T. (2013, December 22). Good poor, bad poor. *New York Times,* SR11.

Friedman, T. L. (2014, Jan. 5). Compromise: Not a 4-letter word. *New York Times,* SR11.

Gabriel, T. (2013, December 29). Uneasy time for Democrats in W. Virginia. *New York Times,* A1, A22.

Hulse, C. (2014, April 26). In Washington, even an accord ends in discord. *New York Times,* A1, A3.

Krauthammer, C. (2013, November 17). Why "Obamacare" panics liberals. *Birmingham News,* 4F.

Landler, M., & Shear, M. D. (2014, April 18). Signups exceed Obama's goal for health act. *New York Times,* A1, A15.

Krugman, (2013, December 6). Obama gets real. *New York Times,* A31.

Krugman, (2014a, Jan. 24). The populist imperative. *New York Times,* A25.

Krugman, (2014b, April 11). Health care nightmares. *New York Times,* A21.

Martin, J. (2013, November 2). G.O.P. arm warns firm targeting incumbents. *New York Times,* A14.

Martin, J. (2014a, January 31). Super PAC is formed in Mississippi to protect 6-term senator in G.O.P. primary. *New York Times,* A14.

Martin, J. (2014b, February 8). Lacking house, senator renews his Kansas ties. *New York Times,* A1, A11.

Martin, J. (2014c, April 5). Tea Party aims at incumbents, but falls short. *New York Times,* A1, A3.

Martin, J. (2014d, April 20). Republicans see political wedge in common core. *New York Times,* A1, A16.

Martin, J. (2014e, June 1). Sensing Tea Party weakness, mainline Republicans flex their muscle. *New York Times,* A19.

Martin, J. (2014f, June 11). In Virginia upset, Tea Party bests top Republican. *New York Times,* A1, A16.

Martin, J., & Parker, A. (2014, March 16). Obama factor adds to fears of Democrats. *New York Times,* A1, A20.

Moore, M. T. (2013, October 17). Cory Booker wins Senate seat in N. J. *USA Today,* 3A.

Nielson, C. M. (2014, April 3). Alabama businessman fueled lawsuit. *Wall Street Journal,* 4A.

Page, S. (2013, November 15). Health law shakes presidency. *USA Today,* 1A-2A.

Parker, A. (2013, November 24). In immigration battle, advocates for overhaul single out Republicans. *New York Times,* A19.

Parker, A. (2014a, February. 7). Democrats aim for a 2014 more like 2012 and 2008. *New York Times,* A14.

Parker, A. (2014b, April 13). North Carolina shows strains within G.O.P. *New York Times,* A1, A18.

Parker, A. (2014c, April 18). In a political "arms race," attack ads give way, a little, to a sunnier side. *New York Times,* A14.

Parker, A. (2014d, April 25). Democratic candidates grow more vocal in supporting health law. *New York Times,* A13.

Parker, A., & Martin, J. (2014, June 21). G.O.P. Senator courts blacks in Mississippi primary race. *New York Times,* A1, A14.

Peters, J. W. (2013, May 31). Sizing up a president as a midterm election target. *New York Times,* A13.

Peters, J. W. (2014, April 18). G.O.P. discovers useful voter outreach tool: Gun sweepstakes. *New York Times,* A12, A14.

Peters, J. W., & Dewan, S. (2014, June 15). For businesses and the G.O.P., a Cantor effect. *New York Times,* A1, A16.

Peters, J. W., & Hulse, C. (2014, April 6). To hit back at Kochs, Democrats revive tactic that hurt Romney. *New York Times,* A1, A19.

Powers, K. (2013, May 14). Republicans lose credibility by constantly crying wolf. *USA Today,* 7A.

Richtel, M., & Confessore, N. (2014, February 9). The G.O.P., wooing the wired. *New York Times,* BU1, BU3.

Rove, K. (2014, April 3). Why the Senate races will soon get ugly. *Wall Street Journal,* A15.

Schwartz, N. D. (2014, May 3). Jump in payrolls is seen as a sign of new optimism. *New York Times,* A1, B2.

Shear, M. D. (2014, May 3). Democrats struggle to turn economic gains into political ones. *New York Times,* A12.

Steinhauer, J. (2013, November 30). As fund-raisers in Congress, women break the cash ceiling. *New York Times,* A1, A11.

Weisman, J. (2013a, May 17). G.O.P., energized, weighs how far to take inquiries. *New York Times,* A1, A12.

Weisman, J. (2013b, November 1). Health law woes have Democrats feeling anxious. *New York Times,* A1, A15.

Weisman, J. (2013c, November 17). In fracas on health care, some Democrats feel exposed. *New York Times,* A1, A19.

Weisman, J. (2014a, April 11). Radio clip shows different side of Republican Senate challenger in Mississippi. *New York Times,* A17.

Weisman, J. (2014b, May 3). Candidate of Tea Party in Kentucky hits snag. *New York Times,* A10.

Weisman, J. (2014c, June 13). Cantor loss may temper House leaders. *New York Times,* A18.

Weisman, J., & Parker, A. (2014, February 8). Boehner is hit from the right on immigration. *New York Times,* A1, A10.

West, (2013, March 24). Republican National Committee: Party needs an overhaul. *Birmingham News,* 23A.

Wolf, R., & Schouten, F. (2014, April 3). Court hands more cash to campaigns. *USA Today,* 1A-2A.

THIRTEEN

2016 Election

The 2016 election was full of surprises and contradictions, so many that its plot likely would not have worked as a piece of fiction because it would have been too hard to believe. Consider these snippets:

- The Republican nominee wasn't really a Republican, nor really a conservative. He chose to run as a Republican simply because it offered an easier path to the nomination.
- That nominee was a billionaire who was better known as a television celebrity than for any political achievements.
- The Republican nominee refused to support other Republican candidates, but he won the party's nomination anyway.
- The main opponent of the leading Democratic contender was not even a Democrat, but an Independent socialist who mounted an effective campaign that surprised party leaders.
- The Republican nominee's initial announcement was greeted with laughter and jokes, with one New York newspaper's headline reading, "Bozo the Clown announces for president."
- Pundits, almost universally, tagged the Republican as the probable loser, and most pre-election polls supported that conclusion. He won anyway.
- The Republican victory surprised even the winner. On election day, his campaign leaked information to the news media that they expected it to be a long night.

Overall, columnist Maureen Dowd (2016) may have captured it best in her book, *The Year of Voting Dangerously*. It all was enough to make serious political junkies scratch their heads or throw up their hands in frustration. In essence, everything that experts had taught each other failed to predict what happened in 2016. Even worse, they couldn't even explain it well. The simple explanation was that angry white voters had risen up in defiance of political norms to express their frustration with the system. In the process, they damaged that system even further. Entering the 2016 election, the animosity between Democrats and Republicans was at an all-time high. When the election was over, that animosity had been joined by new fights between establishment Republicans and the rebellious, populist wing of the party that led the election of Donald Trump.

THE EARLY DAYS OF THE TRUMP CAMPAIGN

Donald Trump ran as a candidate in a party that was already facing serious internal issues. John Boehner entered 2015 as Speaker of the House and thus was supposedly a major leader within the GOP. In reality, he faced a rebellion within the House from Tea Party candidates who had first been elected in 2010. Their brand of conservatism was too much for Boehner, who was himself considered a strong conservative. By September of 2015, Boehner had had enough and made plans to resign from the Speaker's position (Steinhauer, 2015; Hulse, 2015). As the *New York Times* wrote, "Mr. Boehner reportedly thought he could survive a leadership challenge only by accepting Democratic support. A party stalwart, he quit instead ("Speaker Boehner . . . ," 2015, A26). Steinhauer added, "His downfall again highlighted the sinewy power of a Republican power faction whose anthem is often to oppose government action. It also made vivid the increasingly precarious nature of a job in which the will and proclivity of a politically divisive body must be managed" (A1).

THE REPUBLICAN PRIMARIES

The Republican primaries eventually had 17 candidates seeking the nomination, but the one who appeared to be an early favorite was former Florida governor Jeb Bush, since he started with high name identification and could raise significant campaign funds (Confessore, 2015). Businessman Donald Trump had also entered the campaign, but his approach to campaigning was such that some pundits believed it increased the subdued Bush's chances of winning. As Wilkinson (2015) wrote, "Trump's bombast allows Bush to win votes by showing restraint." And, he added, "Bush isn't the type to run a race with abandon. Trump is enabling him to run with extra restraint" (12A).

Some of the other candidates looked like potential problems for the Republican establishment. Ben Carson was one such candidate. As Rutenberg (2015) wrote, "His chances of victory are minuscule, but he and other hard-right candidates are a giant headache for the G.O.P. in the 2016 primaries" (43). His problem, as Douthat (2015) noted was that, "Carson . . . is running a more content-free campaign. Like Trump, he's underinformed and prone to wild rhetorical flights. . . . He's offering a collection of pieties and crankery, mostly his candidacy is just about the man himself" (SR11).

The first Republican debate was held in August 2015 with 15 of the 17 candidates participating. No clear winner emerged, but there were some obvious losers. Losers included Jeb Bush who "seemed nervous and scored . . . (only when he attacked a member of the media)," Kentucky senator Rand Paul "seemed tired . . . (and it was hard to remember when he was the flavor of the month)," and Wisconsin governor Scott Walker ("showed himself lacking only what all presidential candidates must lack: modesty") (Simon, 2015). Some pundits considered Ohio governor John Kasich the Republicans' best choice and the candidate most likely to beat Hillary Clinton, but many voters simply didn't know who he was (Bruni, 2015).

Texas senator Ted Cruz's entry into the campaign provided the far right with a candidate, a fact emphasized by Cruz choosing the ultra-conservative Liberty University to make the announcement of his candidacy (Dionne, 2015). Former Arkansas governor Mike Huckabee entered the race for his second campaign for president (Tumulty, 2015), relying on support from conservative Christians (Will, 2015), but he received little support. Former business executive Carly Fiorina was the only woman candidate among the competitors, relying on her business background to help her stand out from the crowd (Jackson, 2015). Although she started slow, she gained enough support to participate in the second Republican debate (Parker & Gabriel, 2015). Senator Paul entered the race with high name identification (Page, 2015a), but he was hindered by problems in raising money (Mascaro, 2015). Businessman and reality TV star Donald Trump entered the campaign, promising to spend his own money to win, but his campaign was initially met with skepticism (Egan, 2015b; Smith, 2015). Rick Santorum thought his earlier effort might give him an edge (Page, 2015b). Other candidates included Louisiana governor Bobby Jindal (Thomas, 2015), former New York governor George Pataki (Burns, 2015), former Texas governor Rick Perry (Fernandez, 2015), New Jersey governor Chris Christie (Barbaro, 2015; Rieder, 2015a), Florida senator Marco Rubio (Parker, 2015), and Wisconsin governor Scott Walker (Krauthammer, 2015).

Most were out of contention before 2016 even began. By the first Republican debate in January, only seven serious candidates remained; these included the six strongest competitors [including] Bush, Cruz, Kasich, Christie, Rubio, and Trump (Page, 2016a). However, that debate included an infamous exchange between Trump and moderator Megyn Kelly over women's issues; for days following the debate, Trump attacked her as being unfair to him (Jackson, 2016a; Rieder, 2016b). Meanwhile, Trump's appeal grew, including an endorsement from former

vice-presidential candidate Sarah Palin (Rieder, 2016a), despite opposition from establishment Republicans (e.g., Wehner, 2016).

Trump was expected to win in the Iowa caucuses in early February,
but Ted Cruz captured an upset win while Rubio finished second (Jackson, 2016b). Meanwhile, Bush was hurt by a poor showing in Iowa (Martin & Parker, 2016) and a fourth-place finish in New Hampshire (Schout-
en, 2016a). He dropped out of the race before the end of February (Reinhard & Ballhaus, 2016). Chris Christie was even less effective and also
dropped out (Symons, 2016), as did Jim Gilmore (Rappeport, 2016a), and
both Rand Paul and Rick Santorum (Parker, 2016). Ben Carson quit the
campaign in early March (Epstein, 2016a). Carly Fiorina soon followed
suit, endorsing Ted Cruz (Epstein, 2016b). Jeb Bush spent more than $100
million in his losing effort before quitting the race ("Big campaign money . . . ," 2016). Marco Rubio also dropped out, leaving Cruz, John Kasich,
and Trump as the final three contenders (Flegenheimer, 2016a).

One major event in the Republican campaign did not involve any of
the candidates. Supreme Court justice Antonin Scalia died unexpectedly,
leaving Republicans with one less vote on the Court. Republicans in the
Senate decided to put a hold on any efforts to confirm anyone to the post
that President Obama might nominate (Harris & Herszenhorn, 2016). Obama named Merrick Garland to the post, which merely sparked a fight in
the Senate (Shear, Davis & Harris, 2016).

Meanwhile, Trump was solidifying his hold on the Republican nomination, using a message that included building a wall along the Mexican
border (Preston, Rappeport & Richtel, 2016), conspiracy theories (Haberman, 2016), celebrity (Crovitz, 2016), and appeals to racism (Mahler,
2016), while refusing to release his tax returns as had other candidates
(Eder & Cohen, 2016). Blow (2016a) wrote that "Trump has used a toxic
mix of bullying and bluster, xenophobia and nationalism, misogyny and
racism, to appeal to the darker nature of the Republican Party" (A19).
Some of his ideas were unconventional, such as his proposal to reduce
the national debt by negotiating partial payments with those who held
that debt (Appelbaum, 2016) and another suggestion to simply print
more money to cover the debt (Burns, 2016b). However, his impending
success led to an increase in voter registration by Hispanics (Preston,
2016).

Regardless, Trump seemed poised to secure the nomination despite
lack of support from some key Republicans, including Speaker of the
House Paul Ryan (Steinhauer & Burns, 2016) and former opponents Jeb
Bush and Lindsey Graham (Burns, 2016a). Overall, his candidacy was
viewed as potentially unraveling the establishment side of the Republican Party (Healy & Martin, 2016). Meanwhile, other Republican candidates were caught in a quandary of trying to decide whether it was in
their best interests to support his campaign or oppose it (Kraushaar,
2016). That's one reason Douthat (2016) called Trump's campaign "an

invitation to chaos that must be resisted" (SR11). Similarly, Blow (2016) wrote, "Trump is nothing but bad news for his party" (A19). Another Republican wrote that "Our voters, in decisive numbers, picked a guy who embarrasses us" (Wallace, 2016, A25). Rutenberg (2016a), conversely, blamed the media, including himself, for unwittingly aiding in Trump's campaign; "Wrong, wrong, wrong, to the very end, we got it wrong," he wrote (B1). Krugman (2016a), however, argued that Trump was just a symptom of a bigger problem within the Republican Party. "The important thing to realize . . . ," he wrote, "is that when Mr. Trump talks nonsense, he's usually just offering a bombastic version of a position that's widespread in his party" (A19). Still, even as the controversy over Trump's treatment of women swirled, evangelicals largely maintained their faith in the candidate (Zoil, 2016).

However, the Republican convention got off to a bad start when Melania Trump gave a speech that was heavily plagiarized from a speech given by Michelle Obama (Horowitz, 2016).

THE DEMOCRATIC PRIMARIES

The Democrats planned to hold their nominating convention in Philadelphia, the city of brotherly love (Gabriel, 2015). Hillary Clinton was easily the leading candidate, despite a lingering problem with emails while she was secretary of state (Healy, Martin & Haberman, 2015; Robinson, 2015; Rieder, 2015b). Unfortunately for her, the FBI reopened the investigation in late October, less than two weeks before the election (Goldman, et al., 2016). Still, she was raising significant campaign funds, enough to discourage many opponents (Confessore, Haberman & Cohen, 2015). Her opponents included former Maryland governor Martin O'Malley (Haberman, 2015; Horowitz, 2015), former senator Jim Webb (Haberman & Rappeport, 2015), and Lincoln Chaffee, who was the first to drop out (Rappeport, 2015b). Her toughest challenge, though, came from a candidate who wasn't even a Democrat, socialist Bernie Sanders (Rappeport, 2015a). His campaign effectively pushed Clinton to establish positions that were more liberal than her campaign had planned (Mullany, 2015). Still, Clinton's only serious competition looked to be Vice President Joe Biden; when Biden decided not to run, her path was clear (Przybala, 2015).

Clinton was still the front-runner, primarily due to her ability to raise money. By the end of 2015, she had already amassed a war chest that exceeded $110 million (Chozick, 2016a). She also received a number of crucial endorsements, including that of Planned Parenthood. The organization's endorsement was the first in the history of the organization (Chozick, 2016b). Clinton also had the tacit support of President Barack Obama, support that also included access to his network of foot soldiers (Landler, Horowitz & Chozick, 2016). However, she got a scare when

Sanders ran a tight race against her in the Iowa caucuses and in other states (Przybala, 2016). Sanders also made news with a visit to the Vatican in April (Tau, 2016). But Sanders' surprising strength as a candidate merely delayed Clinton's securing of the nomination. Ultimately, he could do nothing to stop her.

The Democratic Convention was only a formality, but the highlight of its speeches came from an unexpected speaker. Khizr Kahn, with his silent wife by his side, American Muslims whose son died a hero's death in the Middle East, spoke. Kahn stirred up the convention when he offered to loan his copy of the U.S. Constitution to Donald Trump; Trump responded by attacking Kahn, and by implication, his son (Cohen, 2016; Oppel, 2016). Michelle Obama was also a popular speaker at the convention in Philadelphia (Hohmann, 2016). Meanwhile, Meg Whitman, a major Republican contributor, announced that she would raise money and campaign for Clinton (Martin, 2016b). Clinton was also widely viewed as the winner of the second debate. As Blow (2016b) wrote, "Hillary Clinton delivered a devastating kidney punch, calling out Trump for his sexist, bigoted comments about a Miss Universe, Alicia Machado" (A23). Editorial and opinion writers came out strongly for Clinton, including one who wrote about Trump, saying "Protect the Oval Office from a thug who lies and cheats" (Cohn, R., 2016, A21).

THE GENERAL ELECTION

In May, Clinton held a 13-point lead in the polls over Trump (Hafner, 2016), raising the possibility that she would be an easy winner in the general election despite the fact that the FBI was investigating her for possibly sending classified information through unsecured emails (Lichtblau & Flegenheimer, 2016). However, Page (2016b) predicted that Trump could win by winning five key states: Arizona, North Carolina, Florida, Ohio, and Pennsylvania. Trump eventually would win all five. In July, her email troubles seemed to move to the backburner when the FBI announced they would not to indict her on any misconduct, despite severe criticism of her actions by FBI director James Comey (Miller, 2016). She solidified the party's ticket by naming Virginia senator Tim Kaine as her running mate (Flegenheimer, 2016b). However, questions about Clinton's health arose in September when she needed help being escorted from a public ceremony (Lezer, 2016), and an announcement of a diagnosis of pneumonia soon followed (Altman, 2016).

Questions about foreign donations to the Clinton Foundation also became an issue; Clinton responded by saying such donations would not be accepted if she won the presidency (Chozick, 2016d). Meanwhile, in an indication of the negative images of both candidates, one pundit described Clinton as "The bitch America needs" (Zeisler, 2016, SR2).

Another prediction was Shouten's (2016b) contention that the campaign would involve an extensive amount of negative attacks. Trump, for example, attacked Clinton's character, calling her "crooked Hillary" (Healy, 2016a, A15). Clinton, meanwhile, labeled Trump as unqualified to be president (Chozick, 2016c) and attacked him as being dangerous for the economy (Chozick & Flegenheimer, 2016). Bernie Sanders joined Clinton in some campaigning in an effort to get his supporters behind the Democratic ticket (Collins, 2016), while President Obama endorsed Clinton in another effort to unite the party (David & Martin, 2016).

Trump, meanwhile, continued his controversial campaign. That included criticizing the judge in one of his civil cases for being a Mexican (Rappeport, 2016b) and vowing to ban Muslims from entering the country (Martin & Burns, 2016a). He also faced a civil lawsuit on charges that his Trump University engaged in fraud in recruiting students (Martin, 2016a), and he sent out a tweet with an anti-Semitic image in it (Haberman, Barbaro, & Martin, 2016). Trump's messages were so controversial that Sexton (2016) argued that the candidate's rallies were "safe havens" where his supporters could voice their own opinions on racism and other issues. Such tactics led columnist Thomas Friedman (2016) to write, "If a party could declare moral bankruptcy, today's Republican Party would be in Chapter 11" (A19). Conservative columnist David Brooks (2016a), commenting on Trump, also had a negative view, writing "His is a political campaign charging ever more wildly out of control. And no, he cannot be changed. . . . he lacks the inner equipment that makes decent behavior possible" (A25). Similarly, Burns and Haberman (2016) wrote, "He has repeatedly signaled to his advisers and allies his willingness to change and adapt, but has grown only more volatile and prone to provocation since then" (A1).

Trump's strategy for winning the election essentially amounted to increasing turnout among white voters (Cohn, 2016a), particularly white voters without a college degree (Cohn, 2016b). Thus, Confessore (2016) wrote, Trump has "opened the door to assertions of white identity and resentment in a way not seen so broadly in American culture in over half a century" (A1). Discouraged Republicans even talked about replacing Trump at the top of the ticket (Peters, 2016). One noncontroversial action by Trump was the selection of Indiana governor Mike Pence as his running mate (Healy 2016b). He also made a controversial statement that gun owners should handle Clinton (Corasaniti & Haberman, 2016).

Trump spent much of his time under the premise of the hostile media effect, i.e., that the media was being unfair to his campaign. His anti-media campaign was particularly intense against the *Washington Post*, with him eventually banning reporters from that newspaper from attending and covering his rallies (Grynbaum, 2016; Burns & Corasaniti, 2016).

LOOSENING THE REINS OF CIVILITY

Immigration was a major issue for both parties, with Republicans arguing for restricting it and even deporting some residents, while Democrats tried to increase voter registration efforts among legal immigrants (Calmes, 2015). Trump met with the president of Mexico in an effort to soften his image on the topic, but the two men had differing memories of their discussion about building a wall along the border (Ahmed & Malkin, 2016; Jackson & Agren, 2016). Republicans also campaigned on killing the health care law known as ObamaCare (Egan, 2015a).

However, the bigger fear among Democrats was that of money. The Koch brothers alone were prepared to spend nearly $900 million on behalf of Republican candidates (Schouten, 2015). Funds from another donor, Sheldon Adelson, could push the total to more than a billion dollars (Wickham, 2015). And, Trump got a boost when he gained the backing of evangelical Christians, even though he is not a religious person (Wehner, 2016). Still, Trump was expected to lose because, as Roller (2016) wrote, "You can't be openly racist and run for president" (SR5).

The first debate came and went with Trump appearing to be underprepared, while Clinton gave a steady performance (Shear & Healy, 2016; Poniewozik, 2016). By then, Trump was describing the election as a rigged system in which he might not concede if he lost (Edsall, 2016). Then, just before the second debate, a tape was discovered that had Trump bragging about groping women, something he claimed he could do because he was a celebrity (Healy & Rappeport, 2016). That topic became a major issue at the second debate, with some Republican women deserting Trump after it became public (Martin & Burns, 2016b). In September, at a Democratic fund-raiser Clinton said that half of Trumps' followers were a "basketful of deplorables," which probably did not help her campaign.

The *New York Times* released one year of Trump's tax returns, a form that showed he paid no taxes that year. Clinton took advantage of that by pushing the issue in their debate (Chozick, 2016e). In early October, most voters agreed with Clinton. More than 60 percent said that Trump did not have the temperament to be president (Blow, 2016b). Rutenberg (2016b) summarized the media's view of Trump when he noted that Trump got the Republican nomination with the aid of the media, but added, "Now that same environment could very well be the thing that destroys it" (A1).

Less than two weeks before the election, FBI chief Comey stated that new emails were found involving Clinton. Despite the fact that there were no specific allegations, the announcement surely hurt Clinton's campaign. Within days, Comey stated there was nothing new. Now a couple of days before the election, his pronouncement was far too late to prevent damage to Clinton.

In the end, of course, Trump won by sweeping North Carolina, Florida, Pennsylvania, Ohio, Michigan, and Wisconsin. The victory surprised Democrats, Republicans, and even Trump himself. The post-election autopsy included a great deal of blame and finger-pointing. The number of racist acts by individuals immediately increased (Bacon, 2016). American Nazis found themselves closer to a president than ever before, and many put away their swastikas in an effort to become even more mainstream (Kovaleski, et al., 2016). Schoenfeld (2016) wrote that "Trump has exposed GOP cowardice, right-wing hypocrisy, and working-class anger" (7A). Stephen Prothero seemed to capture the mood of Democrats when he seemed to shrug his shoulders and wrote, "Oh well, so much for American exceptionalism" (7A). Other voters were more concerned about the impact of new leadership on them personally, such as those who faced a loss of health insurance if ObamaCare were repealed (O'Donnell, 2016). Such concerns were understandable, but it did nothing to change the facts. Donald Trump had won the presidential election and nobody really knew what to expect.

CONCLUSIONS

Columnist Paul Krugman (2016b) summarized his view of the 2016 election when he wrote, "Tribalism is the opposite of patriotism" (A23). Similarly, David Brooks (2016b) wrote, "Politics is no longer about argument or discussion; it's about trying to put your opponents into the box of the untouchables." And, he added, "Donald Trump didn't invent this game, but he embodies it" (A19). Hochschild (2016), in a study of the Tea Party in Louisiana, described the voters who make the difference as angry white voters who were both victims and soldiers in a class war in America. They had been marginalized by flat or falling wages, victims of rapid demographic change, and they blamed a liberal culture that looks down at their religion and patriotism (Hickson & Powell, 2016). The result was one of the most bitter campaigns in modern presidential elections.

The hope that the 2016 campaign might reduce that problem was futile. If anything, tribalism and intra-party conflict increased, and the nation grew more divided. Trump's campaign relied on fear as a motivator, and it worked; voters who normally would have paid him little attention turned out in droves to support his candidacy. And the problems of a divided nation grew worse, not better.

The childishness was modified in that, instead of Republicans and Democrats fighting over "toys," Trump engaged those who were fed up with both sets of kids—the Democrats and the establishment Republicans. Voters supported Trump with a Republican Senate and House and most likely Supreme Court. To some extent, the issue becomes whether one man (an outsider), can get anything done in a town whose habitual infighting has been the modus operandi for years, for decades. Many American people fear that the pre-school may be turned into anarchy or despotism.

For Trump, his use of political incorrectness grasped those alienated voters. He focused on fear—of Muslims, of Hispanics, of blacks—and promised to "fix" the consumerism issues. He opposed the status quo to win the election. The question for everyone has become, "Where do we go from here?"

REFERENCES

Ahmed, A., & Malkin, E. (2016, September 1). Mexican leader disputes Trump on border wall. *New York Times*, A1, A17.

Altman, L. K., MD (2016, September 19). Doctors weigh in on Clinton's health after a pneumonia diagnosis. *New York Times*, A12.

Appelbaum, B. (2016, May 7). Trump floats idea to cut the national debt: Get creditors to accept less. *New York Times*, A10.

Bacon, J. (2016, November 11). Rise in racist acts follows election. *New York Times*, 1A-2A.

Barbaro, M. (2015, November 30). Chasing endorsements, Christie showers New Hampshire with calls and texts. *New York Times*, A13.

Big campaign money will be back (2016, March 1). *New York Times*, A26.

Blow, C. M. (2016a, May 9). G.O.P. has only itself to blame. *New York Times*, A19.

Blow, C. M. (2016b, October 3). Donald Trump: Terroristic man-toddler. *New York Times*, A23.

Brooks, D. (2016a, August 5). The wet noodle Republicans. *New York Times*, A25.

Brooks, D. (2016b, September 2). Identity politics run amok. *New York Times*, A19.

Bruni, F. (2015, August 30). The real threat to Hillary Clinton. *New York Times*, SR3.

Burns, A. (2015, May 29). Pataki adds a socially liberal voice to the race for G.O.P. nomination. *New York Times*, A16.

Burns, A. (2016a, May 7). Rift grows wide as Republicans abandon Trump. *New York Times*, A1, A10.

Burns, A. (2016b, June 11). What a to-do list might look like for Clinton now. *New York Times*, A12.

Burns, A., & Corasaniti, N. (2016, August 13). Trump's other campaign foe: The 'lowest form of life' news media. *New York Times*, A10.

Burns, A., & Haberman, M. (2016, August 14). The failing inside mission to tame Trump's tongue. *New York Times*, A1, A16.

Calmes, J. (2015, January 24). Latino voice on TV news sends shiver over G.O.P. *New York Times*, A11, A13.

Chozick, A. (2016a, January 2). Clinton campaign raised $37 million in last 3 months. *New York Times*, A9.

Chozick, A. (2016b, January 8). Planned Parenthood gives first primary endorsement in its 100 years to Clinton. *New York Times*, A14.

Chozick, A. (2016c, May 20). Clinton declares Trump unqualified for presidency. *New York Times*, A16.

Chozick, A. (2016d, August 19). Donations from abroad would cease, Clinton says. *New York Times*, A12.

Chozick, A. (2016e, October 4). Clinton, seizing on tax returns, says Trump embodies "rigged system." *New York Times*, A12.

Chozick, A., & Flegenheimer, M. (2016, June 21). Clinton to batter Trump as reckless on economy. *New York Times*, A15.

Cohen, R. (2016, May 10). Sadiq Khan vs. Donald Trump. *New York Times*, A21.

Cohn, N. (2016a, June 10). Finding a whiter electorate that opens a path for Trump. *New York Times,* A1, A23.

Cohn, N. (2016b, July 26). The one demographic that Clinton can't seem to win over. *New York Times,* A11-A12.

Cohn, R. (2016, October 4). The Trump possibility. *New York Times,* A21.

Collins, G. (2016, June 9). The Hillary and Bernie road trip. *New York Times,* A21.

Confessore, N. (2015, July 10). Bush outstrips rivals in fund-raising as "Super PACs' swell candidates' coffers." *New York Times,* A18.

Confessore, N. (2016, July 14). Trump mines grievances of whites who feel lost. *New York Times,* A1, A14-A15.

Confessore, N., Haberman, M., & Cohen, S. (2015, October 17). Filings reveal Clinton leads money race. *New York Times,* A1, A13.

Corasaniti, N., & Haberman, M. (2016, August 10). Trump suggests gun owners act against Clinton. *New York Times,* A1, A12.

Crovitz, L. G. (2016, March 14). Donald Trump, celebrity politician. *Wall Street Journal,* A17.

David, J. H., & Martin, J. (2016, June 10). Moving to unite the party, Obama endorses Clinton. *New York Times,* A1, A23.

Dionne, E. J. (2015, March 27). Cruz entry signals fight ahead in GOP. *Birmingham News,* 14.

Douthat, R. (2015, September 20). The Carson illusion. *New York Times,* SR11.

Douthat, R. (2016, May 8). The conservative case against Trump. *New York Times,* SR11.

Dowd, M. (2016). *The year of voting dangerously: The derangement of American politics.* New York: TwelveBooks.

Eder, S., & Cohen, P. (2016, March 1). Cruz and Rubio release tax filings to pressure Trump into doing the same. *New York Times,* A19.

Edsall, T. B. (2016, September 11). The paranoid style in American politics is back. *New York Times,* SR6.

Egan, T. (2015a, February 21). The plot to kill health care. *New York Times,* A19.

Egan, T. (2015b, June 28). A refuge for racists. *New York Times,* SR11.

Epstein, R. J. (2016a, March 3). Carson signals end to his GOP candidacy. *Wall Street Journal,* A6.

Epstein, R. J. (2016b, March 10). Fiorina backs Cruz, slams Trump again. *Wall Street Journal,* A3.

Fernandez, M. (2015, January 16). Perry exits Texas stage making a case for his past, and his future. *New York Times,* A1, A18.

Flegenheimer, M. (2016a, March 17). With Rubio out, Cruz eyes Kasich as new rival. *New York Times,* A17.

Flegenheimer, M. (2016b, July 15). In audition with Clinton, Senator nails his lines. *New York Times,* A15.

Friedman, T. L. (2016, June 8). Dump G.O.P. for a grand new party. *New York Times,* A19.

Gabriel, T. (2015, February 13). Democrats pick Philadelphia for 2016 convention. *New York Times,* A16.

Goldman, A., Rappeport, A., Schmidt, M. S., & Agiuzzo, M. (2016, October 29). New emails found in Weiner inquiry jolt 2016 election. *New York Times,* A1, A12.

Grynbaum, M. M. (2016. June 14). *Washington Post* barred from Trump's campaign. *New York Times,* B6.

Haberman, M. (2015, May 31). O'Malley enters Democratic race for president, pushing image of vitality. *New York Times,* A16.

Haberman, M. (2016, March 1). Trump gives conspiracy theories a conduit into presidential politics. *New York Times,* A18.

Haberman, M., & Rappeport, A. (2015, July 3). Ex-Virginia Senator joins 2016 Democratic campaign. *New York Times,* A12.

Haberman, M., Barbaro, M., & Martin, J. (2016, July 7). In defiant, angry speech, Trump defends picture seen as anti-Semitic. *New York Times,* A16.

Hafner, J. (2016, May 5). Clinton leads Trump by 13%, new poll finds. *USA Today,* 8A.

Harris, G., & Herszenhorn, D. M. (2016, March 2). Obama and G.O.P. senators meet on filling Scalia's seat, to no avail. *New York Times,* A12.

Healy, (2016a, May 17). Little to be off limits as Trump plans attack on Clinton's character. *New York Times,* A15.

Healy, (2016b, July 19). A choice that frees Clinton's hand. *New York Times,* A11, A16.

Healy, P., & Martin, J. (2016, May 8). G.O.P. unravels as party faces Trump takeover. *New York Times,* A1, A19.

Healy, P., Martin, J., & Haberman, M. (2015, August 28). Democrats see an email issue that won't die. *New York Times,* A1, A15.

Healy, P., & Rappeport, A. (2016, October 8). Trump brags on 2005 tape of groping women. *New York Times,* A1, A12.

Hickson, M. III, & Powell, L. (2016, March). It can't be like it used to be: Informality as a contagion of democratization in American culture. *Journalism and Mass Communication, 6,* 146–157.

Hochschild, A. R. (2016). *Strangers in their own land: Anger and mourning on the American right.* New York: New Press.

Hohmann, J. (2016, July 27). First Lady steals the show. *Birmingham News,* A14.

Horowitz, J. (2015, May 1). For ex-mayor's long-shot presidential hopes, Baltimore may be burden. *New York Times,* A20.

Horowitz, J. (2016, July 21). For Ms. Trump's speechwriter, a longtime passion for writing leads into a storm. *New York Times,* A11, A14.

Hulse, C. (2015, September 26). Hard job, getting harder. *New York Times,* A1, A18.

Jackson, D. (2015, May 5). Fiorina to tap politico fatigue. *USA Today,* 8A.

Jackson, D. (2016a, January 28). Debate to-do: Rivals pounce. *USA Today,* 2A.

Jackson, D. (2016b, February 2). Trump upset in Iowa: Rubio is right behind. *USA Today,* 1A, 5A.

Jackson, D., & Agren, D. (2016, September 1). Trump, Mexico politely disagree. *USA Today,* 1A-2A.

Kovaleski, S. E.,Turkewitz, J., Goldstein, J., & Barry, D. (2016, November 11). An alt-right makeover shrouds the swastikas. *New York Times,* A1, A25.

Kraushaar, J. (2016, May 8). Is Trump more dangerous as friend or foe? *New York Times,* SR3.

Krauthammer, C. (2015, March 27). Here's your GOP presidential racing form, first edition. *Birmingham News,* 14.

Krugman, (2016a, May 9). The making of an ignoramus. *New York Times,* A19.

Krugman, (2016b, July 29). Who loves America? *New York Times,* A23.

Landler, M., Horowitz, J., & Chozick, A. (2016, January 23). Their boss stays on the sideline, but Obama aides tilt to Clinton. *New York Times,* A1, A11.

Lezer, L. (2016, August 13). Video puts reporter in midst of latest conspiracy theory. *Birmingham News,* A22.

Lichtblau, E., & Flegenheimer, M. (2016, May 12). F.B.I. chief sees no rush for Clinton email inquiry. *New York Times,* A17.

Mahler, J. (2016, March 1). Trump's message resonates with white supremacists. *New York Times,* A19.

Martin, J. (2016a, June 30). Trump Institute offered get-rich schemes with others' ideas. *New York Times,* A1, A17.

Martin, J. (2016b, August 3). A top Republican donor says she'll vote and raise money for Clinton. *New York Times,* A13.

Martin, J., & Burns, A. (2016a, June 14). Branding Muslims as threats, Trump tosses pluralism aside. *New York Times,* A1, A17.

Martin, J., & Burns, A. (2016b, October 9). Lewd Trump tape a breaking point for many in G.O.P. *New York Times,* A1, A27.

Martin, J., & Parker, A. (2016, February 4). Bush, an also-ran in Iowa, faces burden to show appeal. *New York Times,* A1, A16.

Mascaro, L. (2015, July 19). After sagging in fundraising, Paul reboots campaign. *Birmingham News,* 22A.

Miller, M. (2016, July 8). Comey's abuse of power. *Birmingham News,* A14.

Mullany, G. (2015, May 1). Senator's position on major campaign issues could push Clinton to the left. *New York Times,* A22.

O'Donnell, J. (2016, November 11). Policy experts doubt we'll see full repeal of Obamacare. *USA Today,* 7A.

Oppel, R. A., Jr. (2016, July 30). In tribute to dead son, a lesson in citizenship. *New York Times,* A1, A12.

Page, S. (2015a, April 8). Paul: A familiar name and bonus credibility. *USA Today,* 2A.

Page, S. (2015b, May 28). Sorry, Rick Santorum: no next-guy-in-line this time. *USA Today,* 3A.

Page, S. (2016a, January 15). A smaller field, higher stakes and tougher jabs. *USA Today,* 8A.

Page, S. (2016b, May 5). Five states Trump must win to be president. *USA Today,* 1A, 8A.

Parker, A. (2015, April 18). A greasy hand for Rubio as he visits New Hampshire. *New York Times,* A14.

Parker, A., & Gabriel, T. (2015, August 28). Fiorina, gaining in polls, moves to secure spot in second G.O.P. debate. *New York Times,* A14.

Parker, A. (2016, February 4). Paul and Santorum pull out of G.O.P. nomination race. *New York Times,* A16.

Peters, J. W. (2016, June 10). Talk of a new candidate is still just talk, for now. *New York Times,* A22.

Poniewozik, J. (2016, September 9). In battle of candidates, Lauer is the loser. *New York Times,* A14.

Preston, J. (2016, March 8). To block Trump, Mexicans in U.S. seeking to vote. *New York Times,* A1, A14.

Preston, J., Rappeport, A., & Richtel, M. (2016, May 20). Experts find flaws in Trump plan for wall. *New York Times,* A1, A15.

Prothero, S. (2016, November 22). Oh well, so much for American exceptionalism. *USA Today,* 7A.

Przybyla, H. M (2015, October 22). Now that Biden's bowed out, Clinton strengthens grip. *USA Today,* 1A, 5A.

Przybyla, H. M. (2016, February 2). Clinton, Sanders race goes "down to the wire." *USA Today,* 1A, 5A.

Rappeport, A. (2015a, May 1). Sanders, long-serving independent, enters presidential race as a Democrat. *New York Times,* A22.

Rappeport, A. (2015b, October 24). Chafee drops out of Democratic presidential campaign. *New York Times,* A15.

Rappeport, A. (2016a, February 13). His polling stuck around 0 percent, Gilmore ends a long-shot quest. *New York Times,* A12.

Rappeport, A. (2016b, June 4). Judge faulted by Trump has faced a lot worse. *New York Times,* A12.

Reider, R. (2015a, February 5). GOP hopefuls need to grow a thicker skin. *USA Today,* 2B.

Rieder, R. (2015b, August 20). Clinton dogged by albatross. *USA Today,* 2B.

Rieder, R. (2016a, January 21). With Trump as ringmaster, Palin rejoins media circus. *USA Today,* 2B.

Rieder, R. (2016b, January 28). Trump meets his match in Fox's Kelly. *USA Today,* 2B.

Reinhard, B., & Ballhaus, R. (2016, February 22). Bush campaign proved to be out of step with times. *Wall Street Journal,* A4.

Robinson, E. (2015, March 11). Is Hillary Clinton hiding something in email controversy? *Birmingham News,* 26.

Roller, E. (2016, July 10). Everything I learned from Professor Trump. *New York Times,* SR4-SR5.

Rutenberg, J. (2015, March 22). How do you solve a problem like Ben Carson? *New York Times Magazine,* 43–49.

Rutenberg, J. (2016a, May 9). The Republican horse race is over, and journalism lost. *New York Times,* B1, B5.

Rutenberg, J. (2016b, October 10). Trump, the consummate showman, caught in the Klieg lights. *New York Times,* A1, B3.

Schoenfeld, G. (2016, November 9). A dumpster fire's silver lining. *New York Times,* 7A.

Schouten, F. (2015, January27). The Koch brothers set $889M budget. *USA Today,* 3A.

Schouten, F. (2016a, February 11). Bush donors: Yes! 4th place. *USA Today,* 1A, 5A.

Schouten, F. (2016b, May 18). Mountains of mud set to fly in presidential race. *USA Today,* 5A.

Sexton, J. Y. (2016, July 1). Safe spaces for the right? *New York Times,* A23.

Shear, M. D., Davis, J. H., & Harris, G. (2016, March 17). Obama pick engages Supreme Court battle. *New York Times,* A1, A12.

Shear, M. D., & Healy, P. (2016, September 27). Candidates trade testy exchanges in initial debate. *New York Times,* A1, A12.

Simon, R. (2015, August 5). GOP pack begins to bare its teeth. *Birmingham News,* 12A.

Smith, C. (2015, June 19). Trump's trump: $8.7 billion and an attitude. *Birmingham News,* 13A.

Speaker Boehner quits the arena (2015, September 26). *New York Times,* A26.

Steinhauer, J. (2015, September 26). Boehner to quit, undone by strife with right wing. *New York Times,* A1, A18.

Steinhauer, J., & Burns, A. (2016, May 6). Ryan "not ready" to support Trump, in a rare rebuke. *New York Times,* A1, A15.

Symons, M. (2016, February 11). What went wrong for Christie. *USA Today,* 5A.

Tau, B. (2016, April 9). Sanders will visit the Vatican. *Wall Street Journal,* A4.

Thomas, C. (2015, February 15). Jindal for president? Maybe . . . *Birmingham News,* 20.

Tumulty, K. (2015, May 6). Huckabee to make second bid for president. *New York Times,* 18A.

Wallace, N. (2016, June 30). The G.O.P. waits for Trump to grow up. *New York Times,* A25.

Wehner, P. (2016a, January 14). Why I will never vote for Trump. *New York Times,* A25.

Wehner, P. (2016b, July 5). The theology of Donald Trump. *New York Times,* A23.

Wickham, D. (2015, January 27). Big GOP donor behind Netanyahu flap? *USA Today,* 7A.

Wilkinson, F. (2015, August 5). Is Jeb Bush his party's grown-up? *Birmingham News,* 12A.

Will, G. (2015, May 10). Onward Christian Huckabee. *Birmingham News,* 17A.

Zeisler, A. (2016, September 7). The bitch America needs. *New York Times,* SR2.

Zoil, R. (2016, Oct. 12). Evangelicals defend, deplore Trump. *Birmingham News,* A1, A9.

FOURTEEN

The American Experiment

The American experiment with democracy, over 240 years, has been interesting in many ways. Among them is the issue of the balance of powers among the three branches of government. Most of what we have discussed thus far has concerned conflicts between the legislative and the executive branches. In many years throughout our history, we have elected a president of one party and a legislature of another, which naturally leads to the necessity of compromise if any action is to be taken. The philosophical issue of the power of the judiciary was decided quite early in our history with the case of *Marbury v. Madison*. According to Chief Justice John Marshall: "It is emphatically the province and duty of the judicial department to say what the law is. Those who apply the rule to particular cases, must of necessity expand and interpret the rule. If two laws conflict with each other, the courts must decide on the operation of each" (Lockhart, Kamisar, Choper, & Shiffrin, 1986, 6). In establishing judicial review, and the final review with the Supreme Court, the Court ruled that it is the Supreme Court itself that is the final authority on whether a law passed by the legislature and signed by the executive is consistent with the Constitution. Perhaps not realizing how much power the Court was being allowed, in many cases, it also created the Court as the arbitrator of decisions when the executive and judicial branches were at odds.

THE POWERS OF THE COURT

Realizing that fact, FDR attempted to increase the size of the Court so that he could appoint additional justices, but this never came to fruition. When the Republicans finally took the presidency, Eisenhower appointed Earl Warren of California as chief justice in 1953, although he did not obtain Senate approval until 1954. One of the first cases that the Supreme Court ruled on during Warren's tenure was *Brown v. Board of Education of Topeka, Kansas*. Up to this time, schools all over the country, but especially in the South, operated from a "separate but equal" school system. In many parts of the country, black and white students in the same community attended different schools. In *Brown*, though, the Warren Court ruled that separate but equal was unconstitutional. In large measure, the Court made the ruling because separate was inherently not equal. As a result of that single decision, Earl Warren became the target of many, and in the South, billboards throughout rural areas proclaimed, "Impeach Earl Warren!"

The Public Schools

The *Brown* decision was among the first of many that portrayed a relatively liberal court and caused many to say that the Court was "making rather than interpreting laws." Eisenhower himself was quite dissatisfied with his appointment of Warren, one that the Senate had approved unanimously. It is somewhat ironic that the decision involved a school system in Kansas, but the ruling applied across the country. In some ways, it was a victory for the Republican Party, reinforcing the Party of Lincoln nearly 100 years after the Civil War. But to Southern politicians it was an outrage.

In the antebellum South, slaves were not allowed to learn how to read, and with the *Brown* decision not only would the states be responsible for educating the slaves' black descendants, the states would also have to allow the minority to attend the same schools as the former slave owners' descendants. It should be remembered, though, that the South had a tradition of rebellion, and reaction to this decision would be no different.

Almost immediately following the *Brown* decision, the National Association for the Advancement of Colored People (NAACP) organized students to register to attend formerly all-white schools across the nation. The conflict reached significant proportions in Little Rock's Central High School in 1957 (Campbell & Pettigrew, 1959). The Arkansas governor, Orval Faubus, ordered the state's National Guard to prevent nine African-American students from entering the school, but President Dwight Eisenhower sent U. S. Army regulars to assist the black students. Eisenhower also nationalized the Arkansas National Guard so that they fell under his direction instead of that of Faubus. That was in 1957, but other states, including Mississippi, did not integrate until 1970. That ended the southern rebellion, at least technically. Many southern cities and towns began operating private, segregated, white academies to circumvent the Court's decision. The public, of all races, still had to pay taxes for their public schools, although many resisted in other ways. School bond issues were virtually impossible to pass because white parents were not interested in supporting schools their children did not attend. Still integration became pervasive.

Many citizens began thinking of "integration" as synonymous with "liberal" since the Warren Court was viewed as liberal in many other ways as well. As for minorities, they were mostly pleased with the *Brown* decision, but they knew that black and white issues were far from over. Although Warren was chief justice, no one, including the President, ever expected the Court to go that far.

Religion

In 1962, the Warren Court also ruled that prayer in the schools was unconstitutional. For conservatives, especially those opposed to integration, this was another indicator that the Court was surpassing its just authority. In many states, especially southern states, the rebellion continued on the issue of prayer. Over time, evangelicals continued to oppose the Supreme Court when it appeared to take a liberal stance. Among other tactics, the resistors continued to have prayer during extracurricular events, claiming doing so was not prayer *in the schools*. Protestant ministers delivered prayers at football games in high schools and colleges. Later, the *Roe v. Wade* abortion decision exacerbated the problems between religious conservatives and the Court.

Integration also came to the colleges. Only a few African-American students began attending previously all-white colleges, but they included the University of Mississippi and the University of Alabama, where George C. Wallace stood at the door to prevent a black students' entry. When a member of John Kennedy's attorneys-general's office arrived, Wallace conceded, but he made a public statement in favor of segregation, pronouncing "Segregation now, segregation tomorrow, and segregation forever!"

All of these factors affected conservatives and especially religious conservatives. In 1967, Thurgood Marshall, the African-American attorney who had won the *Brown* case, was appointed to the Supreme Court by Lyndon Johnson.

Following 15 years of the liberal Court, Earl Warren stepped down. Lyndon Johnson attempted to raise Abe Fortas from an associate justice position to chief justice, but a Senate filibuster prevented any action from taking place. The hearings brought forth some ethical problems with Fortas, and he not only lost the chief justice position but also resigned from the associate position. The Republicans and southern Democrats opposed LBJ's appointment of Fortas as chief justice. Fortas was known to be a close friend of Johnson and a pro-civil rights justice. Johnson was near the end of his term. When Fortas stepped down from his associate position, leaving two openings for the next president—the position that Fortas was being recommended for and Fortas' position.

Nixon's Appointments

As it turned out, Richard Nixon appointed four justices during his less than six years in office. Two of them were approved virtually immediately. Warren Burger was approved by the Senate as chief justice. Nixon twice tried to nominate someone to the vacated position of Fortas, but neither gained Senate approval. Nixon then nominated Harry Blackmun, who was confirmed. Whether the "grilling" of Fortas was a factor in the Senate's voting down two nominees to replace Blackmun is open to question, but there probably was a connection. Nixon soon made two other nominations. This time, Nixon "tested the waters" with "leaks" about potential candidates and when the American Bar Association (ABA) disapproved, Nixon instead went for Lewis Powell and William Rehnquist. Both were approved. The Court was moving in an unwavering conservative direction. In 1975, William O. Douglas, the most liberal of the justices, retired. He was replaced by John Paul Stevens.

Despite the fact that the Court was turning conservative, some liberal decisions were made, including allowing the *Washington Post* and the *New York Times* to publish the *Pentagon Papers,* disallowing Nixon to use executive privilege in the Watergate investigation, and notably, two religious decisions. One of them eliminated non-profit status for Bob Jones University, a religious institution, and the other allowed for abortion in the *Roe v. Wade* case. While it was the Burger Court that decided *Roe v. Wade,* most people dissociate the decision from a relatively conservative court. The vote was 7–2.

Rehnquist became the most conservative of the justices. He replaced Burger as chief justice and soon was joined by Clarence Thomas and Antonin Scalia to form a trio of the three most conservative justices since before FDR. The Rehnquist Court ruled that the state of Louisiana's requiring the teaching of creationism in public schools was unconstitutional because it violated the First Amendment.

Reagan's and G. H. W. Bush's Appointments

During Jimmy Carter's short stint in the White House, there were no vacancies on the Court. When Ronald Reagan became president, he attempted to make the Court even more conservative than it had been. When Lewis Powell retired, Reagan nominated Robert Bork. He was known to be extremely conservative, and it should be remembered that he was one of the few who had attempted to protect Nixon during the Watergate scandal. It is doubtful whether Bork would have been approved anyway, but his association with Nixon and Watergate did not help. Reagan appointed Anthony Kennedy, who was approved. For the most part, Kennedy has been the swing vote in cases that ended in a 5–4 vote. The Bork hearings are considered to be the beginning of uncivil behavior on both sides in regard to Court nominations and, perhaps, in regard to politics in general.

When Thurgood Marshall retired in 1991, President George H. W. Bush had an opportunity to increase the conservative nature of the Court. Clarence Thomas was his nominee. The Clarence Thomas hearings in the Senate Judiciary Committee were filled with controversy. George H. W. Bush wanted to appoint a conservative, but he was reluctant to present another white man for the Court. In Clarence Thomas, Bush found what he needed, a native southerner who was African American and conservative. Most of the controversy came from accusations made by Anita Hill, a former employee of Thomas' who claimed she was sexually harassed by Thomas. Liberals were concerned about Thomas' views on affirmative action and abortion. In other words, the issues remained about abortion and race. While all of the controversy was there, Thomas was approved anyway, by a vote of 52–48.

LBJ's appointment of Thurgood Marshall in 1967 was the last Democratic appointment to the Court until the Clinton Administration—for 25 years, all of the appointments were made by Republican presidents. This "monopoly" of conservative appointments to the Court was somewhat equivalent to FDR's being elected four times. During the FDR–Truman administrations, all of the justices were replaced, and some were replaced more than once (Lockhart, et al., 1986, Appendix A, 5). The Court was completely replaced by Republican presidents during the years 1967–1993.

The Rehnquist Court was responsible for the final decision regarding the G.W. Bush–Al Gore election in 2000. The Court ruled that Florida could not change its own rules about allowing for a recount. To the Court, the issue was about due process. The decision was not a straight-party vote. To Democrats it was about the presidency. The state of Florida was the final outstanding issue in the election, and opponents of the decision claim that the conservative court decided who would be president. But if we go back to *Marbury v. Madison*, the Supreme Court had created itself as the final authority. That notion has never been subsequently challenged except in the court of public opinion. Gore won the popular vote, even with the initial results from Florida, but this was an exception to most elections in that the winner of the popular vote and the electoral vote were different.

Despite Democrats' concerns about unfairness and their questioning the authority of the election ever being considered in the Supreme Court, they did learn that appointments to the Supreme Court were critical in deciding who runs the country. It is likely that all Supreme Court nominees will undergo even more questioning in the future, perhaps even more than the Bork nomination.

Recent Court Problems

In 2016, Antonin Scalia suddenly died. This created a vacancy for President Obama. Now two of the strongest three conservatives on the Court were gone, which meant, in all probability, the next appointee would be the key in any 5–4 decisions. Scalia died in February, almost a year before the next president would be elected. However, recognizing the importance of the position, Republicans vowed not to consider Obama's recommendation, arguing that the American people should decide in the next election in November.

This would be Obama's third nomination, as many as Reagan made to create the most conservative court ever. According to Eastwood and Ma (2016), Democrats were in the majority on the Court only from about 1960 to 1976. Conservatives have ruled longer than that period (1977–2017). In the current Court, there are no Protestants. Catholics dominate the Court. All members of the current Court earned degrees from Harvard, Yale, Princeton, or Stanford. Although there have been a few minority and women on the Court, the predominant background of justices has been white males who were educated in Ivy League colleges.

On March 16, 2016, Obama nominated Merrick Garland. Three Republican senators, Jeff Sessions, Mitch McConnell, and Chuck Grassley opposed Garland to the DC Circuit Court, when Garland was nominated by Bill Clinton. Senate leader McConnell continued to oppose Garland in 2016. Even with relatively minor opposition, Garland was approved by a vote of 76–23 to the lower court. All of the negative votes were from Republicans.

Usually court nominees are given an up-or-down vote within 90 days of being nominated. The 2016 Republican strategy to delay a vote is a precedent, and precedents such as this tend to have consequences in the future.

In June, the Supreme Court (composed of eight members) voted against a Texas law that substantially limited the existence of abortion clinics. The decision was 5–3, and observers noted that Anthony Kennedy's vote appeared to having him moving further to the left. That decision may have caused some Republicans who occupy "purple states" to consider Obama's nomination of Garland. A purple state is one that is primarily Democratic, but elected some Republican legislators.

In the summer of 2016, the issue of the federal judicial system became significantly controversial, separately from what was going on with Obama's nominee. Hillary Clinton had been under investigation by the Congress and the FBI for some months for a scandal involving her use of a personal email server when she was secretary of state under Obama. About a week before the FBI was to report on the investigation, Bill Clinton met briefly with the attorney general and had a conversation on the tarmac at the Phoenix, Arizona, airport. The former president stated that it was a friendly conversation (as did Lynch), claiming they did not talk about Hillary's case. Republicans were convinced that Lynch and President Clinton had "made a deal." Lynch later admitted that the cordial meeting was inappropriate (Cillizza, 2016).

The next week, FBI director James Comey announced that although there were difficulties with Clinton's email server, he would recommend to the attorney general that Clinton not be charged. The investigation took months, but all of a sudden things moved swiftly. The attorney general took the recommendation and did not charge Clinton, and then the Republican-controlled House had another investigation about the objectivity of the attorney general and the FBI.

There can be little doubt that the 2016 election cycle will mightily influence society for years to come. Lawsuits related to racial issues and civil rights (especially regarding affirmative action) will continue, as is likely to happen with abortion issues. The issue of states' rights versus the federal government is likely to continue as well.

PARTIES AND IMBALANCE

For many, the 2016 election process has clarified how the system operates. The Constitution does not mention political parties. Political parties are neither part of the Constitution nor the government. The founders of the country certainly intentionally created a system in which it would be extremely difficult for a single person to have enough power to control the country. This is evident in that there are three branches. Each can attempt changes regardless of previous decisions. Judicial review provides this action for the courts to overrule the legislative branch. The President can veto the legislative branch. The legislature can override a veto. With the help of the people and the states, the legislature can amend the Constitution when the Court has made a decision. The only check not in the system is for the executive to override the judicial. However, the executive can operate quite slowly in implementing a court decision, as happened in the civil rights cases. As we have mentioned, the state of Mississippi did not implement the *Brown* decision for more than 15 years.

Political parties threw a wrench into the system, which has become more obvious especially in the 2016 primary elections. Voters discovered that their votes did not "count" as they felt they should count. The Democrats have "superdelegates" who are party officials that carry significant weight in the convention. Bernie Sanders repeatedly complained that the superdelegates had already committed to Hillary Clinton even before the primary season began. These delegates are relatively new to the Democratic system. The 1968 and 1972 elections caused problems for the Democrats, so they created a way to avoid those problems in the future. In addition, both parties have ways of apportioning delegates from the actual votes. In many cases, it has appeared to voters that the apportionment is unfair. Finally, the various state systems in both parties force a candidate to essentially run 50+ campaigns. Some states have primaries, some have caucuses. In some cases, delegates are "chosen" in a manner different from the voting by citizens. In 2016, there was an outcry about the systems in both parties with Donald Trump and Bernie Sanders calling "foul." In fact, though, the parties may run their elections any way they want because the parties are not technically part of the government. Sanders did force some changes in the Democratic Party at the convention, reducing the number of superdelegates. It is a given that the nomination process causes strife in the conventions and the parties for some candidates. Thus, once again, their cries of unfairness essentially amount to this: "I didn't like the way my candidate was treated. We'll get back at them next time."

Once elected, the legislators face the crisis of how to deal with the loyal opposition. This is especially the case when there are splits between the House and the Senate. Over the years, voters have often created such problems by electing senators from one party and House members from another (see Table 14.1).

Interestingly, the number of years that the Democrats and Republicans have been in charge of the White House is relatively the same. When we consider the House and the Senate, the Democrats have been in charge more than double the years of the Republicans. The split houses began with Reagan in 1981–1987, when the Democrats held the House and the Republicans held the Senate. Because the Senate was Republican, Reagan was able to appoint Supreme Court justices with little trouble. The next time was in 2011–2016 when Obama was in the presidency. Only during Obama's first two years were both houses Democratic. In the last two years, both were Republican.

These splits between the houses makes change very difficult. When voters select a president to bring about change, the result is that change is highly unlikely unless the president and both houses are of the same party. It was during Obama's first two years that Obama's health-care program was passed. On numerous occasions, the Republicans challenged Obamacare through the courts knowing that should they pass changes, Obama did not sign them. A two-thirds override of an Obama veto was virtually impossible.

Senate rules also weigh a block higher than a pass. If a bill is challenged, the minority side can start a filibuster, and it takes 60 votes to stop the filibuster. The result of all of these actions means that frequently nothing is passed. In layman's terms: "If I can't get my way, you can't get yours." In brief, this inaction and the confrontations are more like kids playing bumper cars. The goal becomes hitting one another instead of driving around a course. The best analogy for a successful system is to think of the governmental process as these various entities driving cars

Table 14.1.   Executive and Legislative Branches by Party, 1936–2016

President	Party	Years	House Party	Senate	Party Split (Yes or No)
Roosevelt	D	37–39	D	D	No
Roosevelt	D	39–41	D	D	No
Roosevelt	D	41–43	D	D	No
Roosevelt	D	43–45	D	D	No
Truman	D	45–47	D	D	No
Truman	D	47–49	R	R	Yes
Truman	D	49–51	D	D	No
Truman	D	51–53	D	D	No
Eisenhower	R	53–55	R	R	No
Eisenhower	R	55–57	D	D	Yes
Eisenhower	R	57–59	D	D	Yes
Eisenhower	R	59–61	D	D	Yes
Kennedy	D	61–63	D	D	No
Johnson	D	63–65	D	D	No
Johnson	D	65–67	D	D	No
Johnson	D	67–69	D	D	No
Nixon	R	69–71	D	D	Yes
Nixon	R	71–73	D	D	Yes
Nixon/Ford	R	73–75	D	D	Yes
Ford	R	75–77	D	D	Yes
Carter	D	77–79	D	D	No
Carter	D	79–81	D	D	No
Reagan	R	81–83	D	R	Yes
Reagan	R	83–85	D	R	Yes
Reagan	R	85–87	D	R	Yes
Reagan	R	87–89	D	D	Yes
Bush, G H W	R	89–91	D	D	Yes
Bush, G H W	R	91–93	D	D	Yes
Clinton	D	93–95	D	D	No
Clinton	D	95–97	R	R	Yes
Clinton	D	97–99	R	R	Yes
Clinton	D	99–01	R	R	Yes
Bush, G W	R	01–03	R	-	No

Bush, G W	R	03–05	R	R	No
Bush, G W	R	05–07	R	R	No
Bush, G W	R	07–09	D	-	Yes
Obama	D	09–11	D	D	No
Obama	D	11–13	R	D	Yes
Obama	D	13–15	R	D	Yes
Obama	D	15–17	R	R	Yes
SUMMARY	**D-42 R-38**	**D-58 R-22**	**D-54 R-22 T-4**	**Y-42 N-38**	

and meeting at an interaction. At a four-way stop, most of us understand that for anyone to make progress, we must occasionally allow other cars to pass. In the real world, there are few crashes at four-way stops because adults know this. The alternatives are to crash into one another or for all four cars to stop forever.

THE PRESIDENCY

One would anticipate that when the presidency was held by one party and the Congress by another, many of the kinds of blockages that we have discussed would happen more often. To put it in a positive light, one would expect that more would be accomplished when the president and Congress was of the same party. An obvious way of looking at this is to consider vetoes and vetoes overridden.

From Washington through Lincoln, there were few vetoes and only six overrides (Presidential Vetoes, 1789–2015, 2016). But in the next two administrations following the end of the Civil War, Andrew Johnson and U. S. Grant, there were more vetoes than in the previous 100 years. In his first administration, Grover Cleveland vetoed 414 bills. Four years later, during his second term, Cleveland vetoed 170 bills. That is 584 bills that were vetoed during Cleveland's two administrations. Seven of them were overridden (Presidential Vetoes, 1789–2015, 2016).

In recent years, the most vetoes were during the Truman administration (250, with 12 overrides). During the Kennedy, LBJ, Carter, G. H. W. Bush, Clinton, G. W. Bush, and Obama administrations, there were only 183 vetoes and only 12 overrides. In the last 16 years, with G. W. Bush and Obama, only 13 bills have been vetoed, and 6 were overridden.

The numbers are quite small in comparison with other times and other presidents. Interestingly, almost half were overridden. Fourteen of those years, the Republicans controlled Congress. The question becomes whether conflict was actually reduced or whether few controversies made their way to the president (Presidential Vetoes, 1789–2015, 2016).

The most controversial issues were G. W. Bush's foreign policy re-garding Afghanistan and Iraq and Obama's health-care initiative. Serious questioning of the invasion of Iraq has surfaced only in the past few years. The United States still maintains a presence in those countries 14 years later. Obama's health plan was his primary accomplishment during his first two years, when there was a Democratic majority in Congress. Since 2010, there appears to have been little in the way of proposals by either President Obama or the Republican Congress.

Without a majority in the House AND a supermajority in the Senate, little gets done other than the childish criticisms of any proposal by either side. A typical rhetorical response from either side is that "it won't solve the problem." The fact that some proposals may have reduced the prob-lem without solving it appears to land on deaf ears.

Neither vetoes nor overrides have been prominent recently. Accord-ing to DeSilva (2014), during the four-year period of 2011–2014, Congress passed only 218 significant bills. Much of the blame for congressional low productivity is that legislators now spend over half of their time fund-raising for the next election (Smith, et al., 2010). Whereas, money is needed for election purposes, the time must be spent derogating the op-position.

For DeSilva, a writer for the Pew Research Center, the problem is the mentality of those in Congress: "Members of Congress tend to act like harried undergraduates, leaving their hardest assignments till the end of the term and then finishing with a blizzard of activity" (DeSilva, 2014). In a presidential election year, even that is unlikely to occur.

THE MEDIA: FUEL ON THE FIRE

Historically, newspapers were the first to endorse political candidates. As the traditional Fourth Estate, the newspapers kept an eye on the govern-ment and notified the citizenry of the government's fallibilities. For the most part, in the early days, television networks did not formally support candidates or parties. Certainly, CBS was among the first accused of bias when Edward R. Murrow vehemently criticized Joseph McCarthy for the hearings on communism in the 1950s. Although the executives at CBS had supported Murrow in the beginning, eventually Murrow was rele-gated to projects that had little to do with contemporary politics. Neither Murrow nor CBS, however, targeted the Republican Party. In 1988, Dan Rather of CBS, in a live interview, viciously attacked George H. W. Bush for possible involvement in the Iran–Contra affair. Ultimately, Rather was fired for making unsubstantiated allegations against President George W. Bush. In today's world, one might say that everyone is a critic. The Internet allows virtually anyone to establish a newspaper, a radio station, a television station, a film, or a podcast, for endorsing or critiquing candidates. The complexity of such networking sometimes makes it difficult to determine not only who is more objective but also whether there is any truth at all in a statement (Benkler, 2007). To some extent, though, we can trace this problem back to times prior to the Internet's popularity.

Most viewers would see little difference among the traditional networks CBS, NBC, and ABC. It was not until 1996 that Australian entrepreneur Rupert Murdoch hired Roger Ailes as the CEO of the new cable network, Fox News, that the media were caught in battles about relative bias. (Collins, 2004). Ailes used the phrase, "Fair and Balanced," as the motto of the new network. Just because it had the motto does not mean that most observers considered the network either fair or balanced. In 2014, Gabriel Sherman wrote a book in which he accused Ailes of operating Fox with an iron hand and previewed the numerous sexual harassment allegations that have subsequently been directed toward Ailes. In 2016, the Murdoch family decided to replace Ailes at the top of the network (Sherman, 2014).

To counteract the Republican conservative views reported on Fox, NBC created MSNBC as a cable competitor with a left-wing perspective (Entman, 2007). With Fox and MSNBC on opposite ends of the spectrum, the scene was set. Cable stations themselves have created specific audiences for their programs, and the news stations, including CNN, have done no differently.

At the heart of the issue is that media are in the business of doing business. Their goal is not so much to inform the public in an objective manner as it is to make money. Most networks do not intentionally provide false information. They do, however, generate conflict when there is little to support it. They do select segments that fit their purpose of generating conflict. They do focus on horse races in elections at the expense of attempting to notify the public about specific policy issues of the candidates. In a sense, the networks, especially the cable networks, must create controversy and milk it in order to carry what is referred to as "news" on a 24 hour, 7 days a week format. They are like the third child in the family who eggs on the other two to get in a fight. They pour fuel on the fire so to speak, mostly in a campaign to draw more viewers so that they have a rationale to increase charges to advertisers.

The final component is lobbyists, big donors, and money in general. The *Citizens United* case in which the Supreme Court ruled that donating money to candidates' campaigns and gaining general political influence has been the straw that broke the camel's back (Smith, Williams, Powell, & Copeland, 2010). The case has been discussed previously and we will not elaborate specifically on it here. However, the results of the case do impact the media. Television in particular has a vested interest in maintaining the law. Large portions of campaign monies are spent in television advertising. If an election appears to be a runaway for a candidate, it is not to the benefit of television to report it. Voters like horse races, in which both candidates appear capable of winning. When the election outcome appears to be close, more viewers will watch. When nationwide numbers are not close, the media focus on any race that might be close to maintain the horse race mentality. The more viewers, the more advertising. With *Citizens United,* the money is unlimited.

The money issue brings up a significant philosophical and constitutional issue. Capitalism is not part of the Constitution. Although he did not point that out, Bernie Sanders certainly implied it in his 2016 campaign for president. Capitalism and democracy, in fact, may be philosophically at odds when one considers that a dollar counts more than a vote. Decades ago, local politicians bought votes with pints of liquor. Today, the money goes to the media and to the campaigns themselves. There is little doubt that the outrage proclaimed both by Sanders and Trump voters is an outrage directed against rich multi-billionaires who influence political outcomes.

In the 2016 election, the country apparently decided to try to break as many blockades as it could. Trump, a Republican, was elected president. The country voted for a Republican House and a Republican Senate (although the Senate was not a supermajority). Thus, any bill that did not require a supermajority, should have been easy to pass. In addition, Republicans were able to nominate their own candidate to the Supreme Court, giving conservatives a 5–4 majority on many decisions. However, a super majority was still needed to approve the Supreme Court nominee. The Republicans simply changed the rules. What would have been seen as a relatively easy route for legislation, though, was prevented in the first major piece of legislation. In the first attempt for the House to "repeal and replace" Obamacare, the vote had to be called off because they did not have a majority. Why? Because House members were fighting among themselves. Thus, inside party conflicts prevent progress as well.

CONCLUSIONS

When the founders created the United States of America, they knowingly created a system intended to prevent despots from having control. In a sense, they created a "weak" executive branch. But they created a system where checks and balances were all over the place, making it difficult to get things done. When a person had to travel from Georgia to Washington, DC, simply to attend Congress, the world was a much slower place. The executive, the judicial, and the legislative branches were "forced" to cooperate with one another simply to carry on the everyday business of the country.

Despite all of these barriers, significant problems did not occur until almost a century later when the Civil War took place. Whether the Civil War is characterized as an economic war, a war about slavery, a war about states' rights, or a war about cultural differences, it split the nation. That split technically lasted only a few years. But there is little argument against the fact that these issues—especially regarding consumerism and wealth, regarding rich versus poor, regarding states' rights, and regarding how big the government should be and what it should accomplish do go back to the metaphor of children arguing about their toys.

The issue of how large the federal government should be is an interesting one. While both parties occasionally engage in rhetoric that would decrease the size of the federal government, most people believe that Democrats are more willing to decrease the size of the military, and Republicans are more interested in cutting social programs. One way of looking at the issue is to see the total number of federal employees and the total number of military personnel. The U. S. Office of Personnel Management (2014) has provided these numbers from data generated since 1962. The highest total number of federal employees since 1962 is 6,575,000 (1969; LBJ). The highest number of military personnel during the same time period is 3,584,000 in 1968 (LBJ). The highest number of nonmilitary employees was in 1989 (Reagan). In Table 14.2, we have provided data on increases and decreases in numbers of personnel beginning in 1981.

Just during the period of 1981–2014, Republican presidents have added approximately 215,000 federal employees and the Democratic presidents have eliminated 828,000 through 2014. There is no doubt that there are other ways of looking at the size of government. Another way is by looking at the number of government offices. There have been only four cabinet level departments added since 1980. Jimmy Carter added the Departments of Education and Energy. George H. W. Bush added the

Table 14.2. Federal Workforce Since 1962.

President	First Year Personnel	Last Year Personnel	Increase/ Decrease
Reagan	4,982,000	5,289,000	+ 308,000
Bush, G. H. W.	5,292,000	4,931,000	− 261,000
Clinton	4,758,000	4,135,000	− 613,000
Bush, G. W.	4,132,000	4,206,000	+ 174,000
Obama [Through 2014]	4,430,000	4,185,000	− 255,000

Adapted from: U. S. Office of Personnel Management (2015). Historical Federal Workforce Tables.

Department of Veterans Affairs, and George W. Bush added the Department of Homeland Security, following the tragedy of 9/11.

Who started it? If "they" started it, who are "they?" Perhaps it was the audacity of FDR being able to win the presidency four consecutive times that created somewhat of an imbalance. Perhaps it was Kennedy's election in 1960 under questionable voting circumstances and Nixon choosing not to challenge it. Perhaps it was Nixon's Watergate break-in of Democratic headquarters. Perhaps it was Congress' threat to impeach Nixon for his part for the Watergate crime. Perhaps it was southern states being treated like the black sheep of the family for a century and a half.

It could have been the Senate's blocking Supreme Court nominations. It could have been the Republicans forcing Bill Clinton to testify about a court case, stemming from his time as governor of Arkansas that they then used as a basis for impeachment. It could have been about the paradigmatic shift from mostly moderates of both parties to two extremes relatively evenly divided. But ultimately it is based on who owns the toys, and what we have learned is that there is one answer for certain. The American people do not cause any of these problems, unless they get blamed for voting for a split government.

Whether the country is to continue to be great or whether it is to be great again, changes are essential. The sides must first learn how these issues started in the first place. If they do not forgive and forget, we will continue to be mired in petty conflict as we have been since 1980. We must learn that the founders assumed that, although there are barriers and checks and balances, the expectation is that compromise, negotiation, and communication will eventually overcome the difficulties. Those words, "compromise" and "negotiation" are not bad words. They are good ones. Refusing to play with one another ends up affecting not only the two political parties but also 300 plus million American citizens.

REFERENCES

Benkler, Y. (2007). *The wealth of networks: How social production transforms markets and freedom*. New Haven, CT: Yale University Press.

Campbell, E. Q., & Pettigrew, T. F. (1959). Racial and moral crisis: The role of Little Rock ministers. *American Journal of Sociology*, 509–516.

Cillizza, C. (2016, July 4). Bill Clinton and Loretta Lynch made Hillary's e-mail problems look even worse. *Denver Post*. Downloaded from: http://www.denverpost.com/2016/07/04/bill-clinton-and-loretta-lynch-made-hillarys-e-mail-problems-even-worse/.

Collins, S. (2004). *Crazy like a fox: The inside story of how Fox News beat CNN*. Virginia Beach, VA: Portfolio.

DeSilva, D. (2014). Congress continues its streak of passing few significant laws. Downloaded from: http://www.pewresearch.org/fact-tank/2014/07/31/congress-continues-its-streak-of-passing-few-significant-laws/.

Eastwood, J., & Ma, J. (2016, March 16). How Obama's nominee could change the face of the Supreme Court. Downloaded July 10, 2016, from: http://graphics.wsj.com/supreme-court-diversity/.

Entman, R. M. (2007). Framing bias: Media in the distribution of power. *Journal of communication, 57*(1), 163–173.

Lockhart, W. B., Kamisar, Y, Choper, J. H., & Shiffrin, S. H. (1986). *Constitutional law: Cases, comments, questions.* 6th ed. St. Paul, MN: West.

Presidential vetoes, 1789–2015. (2016). Downloaded from: http://www.infoplease.com/ipa/a08011767.html.

Sherman, G. (2014). *The loudest voice in the room.* New York: Random House.

Smith, M. M., Williams, G. C., Powell, L., & Copeland, G. A. (2010). *Campaign finance reform: The political shell game.* Lanham, MD: Lexington.

U. S. Office of Personnel Management (2015). Historical federal workforce tables. Downloaded from: https://www.opm.gov/policy-data-oversight/data-analysis-documentation/federal-employment-reports/historical-tables/total-government-employment-since-1962/.

Index

About the Authors

Mark Hickson III, is professor of Communication Studies at the University of Alabama at Birmingham (UAB). He is a recipient of the Gerald M. Phillips Award for Distinguished Scholarship in Applied Communication Research. He is author or co-author or co-editor of 19 books.

Larry Powell is a professor of communication studies at the University of Alabama at Birmingham (UAB). He specializes in political campaigning and spent 11 years as a full-time political consultant. He is the author or co-author of more than a dozen books.